O MARVELOUS EXCHANGE

*Daily Reflections
for Christmas and Epiphany*

O MARVELOUS EXCHANGE

*Daily Reflections
for Christmas and Epiphany*

John J. McIlhon

A Liturgical Press Book

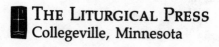
THE LITURGICAL PRESS
Collegeville, Minnesota

Cover by Joshua Jeide, O.S.B.

Nihil obstat: Frank E. Bognanno, *Censor deputatus.*
Imprimatur: ✝ William H. Bullock, D.D., Bishop of Des Moines, Sept. 7, 1990.

Excerpts from the English translation of the non-biblical readings from *The Liturgy of the Hours* © 1974, International Committee on English in the Liturgy, Inc. All rights reserved.

Scripture quotations from the *New American Bible,* copyright © 1970 by the Confraternity of Christian Doctrine, Washington, D.C., and the *New American Bible With Revised New Testament,* copyright © 1986 are reproduced herein by license of said copyright owner. No part of the *New American Bible* may be reproduced in any form without permission in writing. All rights reserved.

1   2   3   4   5   6   7   8   9   10

Library of Congress Cataloging-in-Publication Data

McIlhon, John.
  O marvelous exchange : daily reflections for Christmas and
Epiphany / John J. McIlhon.
      p.   cm.
  Includes bibliographical references.
  ISBN 0-8146-2013-2
  1. Christmas—Meditations.   2. Epiphany season—Meditations.
3. Catholic Church. Liturgy of the hours (U.S., et al.)-
-Meditations.   I. Title.
BX2170.C5M35 1991
242'.33—dc20   91-27880
                                                                CIP

Contents

Preface

A cartoon from a social-justice magazine, *Integrity,* long since out of print, pops into my mind each Christmas. It depicts a board of directors meeting where absolutely nothing is out of place. Seated at a highly polished table is an equally highly polished assembly of executives facing their director with countenances of childlike anticipation. The director greets the assembly with the question, "Now that we're organized, what do we do?"

Yes, every year we find ourselves with the task of organizing Christmas yet uneasy about the feeling that we really don't know what to do with its meaning. That dis-ease begins on December 26, when we begin to dismantle the "organization" of Christmas and, alas, ends with a yawn on an Epiphany whose meaning is beyond us.

This volume of reflections is not a how-to-do-it book. Rather, it invites us to reflect on the mystery of Christ's incarnation not for answers to the question What are we to do? but with light for the question, What are we to be? Christmas and Epiphany endeavor to awaken us to human life's prime purpose. These mysteries of Christ's incarnation enlighten us so that we might see the responsibility of responding to Christ's mission to be the light that enables us to see what we are called to do. Christ's never-ending mission calls us to be transformed into the likeness of Christ's incarnation.

The implications of our transformed personhood to be the manifestation of Christ's presence is the reason I chose this book's title: *O Marvelous Exchange! Daily Reflections for Christmas and Epiphany.* The words "O marvelous exchange" begin the Church's Evening Prayer on the feast of Mary, Mother of God, midway between Christmas and Epiphany. Not by coincidence has Mary's motherhood been chosen as the context of the "marvelous exchange" between our humanity and God's divinity. The gift of her humanity for the gift of Christ in her womb calls all of humanity to the responsibility of manifesting Christ's incarnation.

This fourth book of Word, Reflection, and Questions for Your Reflection, patterned after Lent's *Forty Days Plus Three*, Advent's *God Is with Us*, and Easter's *Fifty Days Plus Forever*, focuses on our responsibility of making real what we say we believe about Bethlehem's marvelous event. We are challenged to look at our humanity for evidence of its exchange for the divinity that has made all of humanity marvelous.

Christians are not called to form an organization to do marvelous tasks for Christ. Christians are called to be the organism that gives evidence of Christ's way, truth, and life. How marvelous to *be* the body of Christ, who longs to be the centerpiece of our lives! It is safe to say that those in whom Christ is the principle of life rarely ask, "Now that we're organized, what do we do?"

Foreword

I am greatly honored for the opportunity of writing the foreword to this book, *O Marvelous Exchange: Daily Reflections on Christmas and Epiphany*. It is a measure of Msgr. John McIlhon's deep concern that the meaning of Christmas and Epiphany be linked to the experiences of our daily lives. The book is enriched by many of his own experiences through which he has been able to link us to deeper meanings of this holy season.

One need not know this book's author very long before sensing his devotion to Christ's "Marvelous Exchange" of the human and the divine. As he celebrates the Eucharist and shows his concern for the people of God, it is apparent that Christ's incarnation is his life's joy. You need only to study a few of his reflections to recognize his deep love for the Word of God and its meaning for human life. The linking of his life to God's Word suggests in remarkable ways the significance of the Christmas-Epiphany season.

I am confident that you will enjoy this book, and more importantly, will appreciate God's gift of Jesus Christ to human life even more. I am grateful for Msgr. John McIlhon's gift on the pages of this book.

Lawrence Breheny
Chancellor
Diocese of Des Moines

Which Day Is Christmas?

WORD

Dearly beloved, our Savior is born; let us rejoice. Sadness should have no place on the birthday of life (St. Leo the Great, pope).[1]

REFLECTION

While I cherish June 6, 1922, my birthday, I have never allowed it to become the meaning of my life. Far more important has been the gift of life delivered to me by my parents, whose love for each other will forever spill over into the identity of my personhood. While midnight of June 6, 1922, ended the day of my birth, the gift of human life will never end.

St. Leo the Great refused to let the alleged date of Christ's birth distract him from its significance for all time. His faith had convinced him that Christ's birthday represented the ongoing "Day" on which all of us have been born into eternal life. St. Leo viewed Christ's acceptance of our humanity as an integral part of human identity. For him, Christ's birth became the "birthday of life" for all who embraced his divine identity as their own, just as he embraced human identity as his own. Christmas, then, celebrates not only that God is with us but also that we are with God.

December 25 is not unimportant, nor is it my intention to erode its importance. Birthdays are valuable when they draw our attention to the meaning of human life and human destiny. However, when the historical date of one's birth becomes detached from life's meaning, birthdays become the pursuit of trivia. Trivia likewise be-

11

comes our pursuit when the birthday of Jesus on December 25 is isolated from the fullest meaning of Christmas. "There is a constant risk that we treat [Christmas] as a birthday pageant. We must be careful to make the distinction between the birthday of Jesus (which Christmas is NOT) and the birth of Christ (which our liturgy shouts 'Hodie,' today). In this festival we celebrate the amazing good news that Christ is born now, to us, in our own flesh and blood."[2]

Throughout Advent we celebrate the good news that God is with us. Christmas is the climax of that Advent message. But Christmas is also the bold assertion that God's being with us is not the final meaning of incarnation. Christ came to be with us so that we might be with God. St. John asserts:

> In the beginning was the Word;
> the Word was in God's presence,
> and the Word was God.
> He was present to God in the beginning.
> Through him all things came into being,
> and apart from him nothing came to be (John 1:1-3).

Christ's being with us was only a part of his ultimate reason for coming into this world. He came to be with us that we might be rejoined to God's reason for creating us. It bears repeating:

> Through him all things came into being,
> and apart from him nothing came to be.

In other words, apart from Christ, human life is meaningless. With God for all eternity, the Word of God was also God's plan for human life's destiny. The Word was sent into the world that God might be marked with the identity of human life. Humanity had always been in the mind of God—long before it was formed. The right to this tremendous dignity of God's parentage was revealed in Jesus, who came to restore it to God's plan for human purpose. No, it is not enough that Christ came to be with us. He came that we might once again be with God, as witnesses of the divine life destined to be reflected in our identity.

The implication of our reentry into the life of God warns us of tensions. If the incarnation stops at "Christ is with us" among some Christians, there may arise the perception that repentance and reform are irrelevant and meaningless. Those who believe only in this perception of the incarnation will be heard saying, "God is on my side." This attitude is both tragic and comic.

Those who believe that Christmas celebrates Christ's human identity in exchange for his divine identity opt for a faith that endeavors to see God's side. The eyes of faith look beyond the appearances of this world so that the gaze of the faithful might be fixed on Christ (see Heb 12:2). God's "side" is justice. This is the justice that sees human purpose in the light of its dignity to be like God. This justice transcends all other appearances of justice. Isaiah declares:

> Not by appearance shall he judge,
> nor by hearsay shall he decide,
> But he shall judge the poor with justice,
> and decide aright for the land's afflicted (Isa 11:3-4).

The "day" of Christmas, then, is much more than December 25. We celebrate the day in history that signaled that the never-ending "day" of humankind's restoration, reform, and renewal of human dignity is at hand. This "day" is the meaning of every day. God is with us and we are with God. These two sides of Christmas exhort us to take seriously St. Leo the Great's cry: "Christian, remember your dignity and now that you share in God's own nature, do not return to your former base condition. Bear in mind who is your head and of whose body you are a member. Do not forget that you have been rescued from the power of darkness and brought into the light of God's kingdom" (St. Leo the Great, pope).[3]

QUESTIONS FOR YOUR REFLECTION

1. How is the fuller significance of Christmas restricted when our sole preoccupation is the historical birth of the infant Jesus?

2. While we believe that Jesus was born on a specific historical date, what is the risk we take with Christ's message of redemption when historical date becomes the sole meaning of Christmas?

3. God is with us and we are with God are two indispensable "sides" of the Christmas mystery. The latter demands responsibility. What is it?

4. When we accept two sides of Christ's incarnation, how does this depth of perception enable us to see the shallowness of "God is on our side"?

Getting the Whole Picture of the Holy Family

WORD

Wives should be submissive to their husbands as if to the Lord (Eph 5:22).

REFLECTION

There is a story about a young parishioner who walked into the church precisely at the moment his pastor cried out: "There is no God!"

Shocked and angered, he immediately walked outside again, determined to give the pastor a piece of his mind.

As the priest approached the rectory after Mass, the angry young man confronted him: "Father," he shouted, "I am sorry I was late for Mass, but I left immediately when I heard you say, 'There is no God!' What kind of nonsense is that?"

Inviting him into the house, the priest quietly opened a Bible to Psalm 14 and asked his visitor to read the first sentence. The young man's face paled as he murmured, "The fool says in his heart, 'there is no God.'" Humiliated and quieted, he remarked, "I see that I got only a part of the picture."

St. Paul frequently gets a piece of many angered minds because they too get only a part of his picture of family life, described in his Letter to the Ephesians. As a result, the Church's presentation of the Holy Family is often impaired by the refusal of some to accept Paul's exhortation, "Wives should be submissive to their husbands," without listening to what it is that St. Paul asks wives to submit themselves. The "submission" St. Paul asks wives to give their husbands is nothing less than Christ's love for the Church. He asks them to submit to the same sacrificial love *husbands* are commanded to witness. "Husbands, love your wives, as Christ loved the church" (Eph 5:25).

The headship of Christ over the Church is not one of domination by force. Rather, it is an outpouring of love, which forms and shapes the integrity of family life. The husband's "head of the family" status is his witness of the sacrificial love Christ displayed on the cross. St. Paul does not hesitate to lay the responsibility of revealing this love squarely on the shoulders of husbands. Nor does he hesitate to ask both wives and children to embrace this love. Why? Because sacrificial love is the only reality that has the capacity to unite the diversities that make up authentic family life.

Obedience is not a call to the passivity of subservience. Rather, obedience envisions the openness of all family members to recognize true freedom, which sacrificial love engenders. Freedom is experienced in homes when a lively sense of belonging and communion have been established. Sacrificial love is the centerpiece of family life because it gives birth to the self-esteem that guarantees freedom. To witness the power of love is to respond to its freeing presence, which, St. Paul claims, begins with husbands.

The duty of obedience residing in mothers and children is not the whole picture. Fathers also bear the responsibility of obedience to St. Paul's imperative that they "love [their] wives, as Christ loved the church." When a man exercises family headship without the obedience of loving his family as Christ loves the church, he does violence to family life. Obedience does not begin with wives and children; it begins with husbands who respond to Christ's obedience to his Father that he restore the family of humankind to its communal kinship with God.

Nor is love the domain only of husbands. It seeks for lodging in all who welcome it by way of obedience. A gift of love ceases to be gift when it is not freely received. No gift has ever matched God's priceless offering of Jesus to Mary. But before God granted Mary the gift of Jesus, he asked for her response, her acceptance, her "submission" to the full presence of that love. He asked Mary to surrender herself to the overshadowing presence of the Holy Spirit. She revealed her obedience when she replied: "I am the servant of the Lord. Let it be done to me as you say" (Luke 1:38). Her obedience to God's gift of love, *in Christ*, enabled Mary and all of humanity to become temples of God's loving presence.

No member of the family, then, is exempt from submission. Fathers, mothers, and children are called to "be submissive" to the love that bonds all of them into communion with God's Trinitarian family. This oneness of Father, Son, and Holy Spirit springs from the love that defines God. St. John the Evangelist could find no words to describe God except "God is love" (1 John 4:16). In the light of that unifying love, Christ obediently embraced family life as his lodging here upon earth. It was in the context of obedience to Joseph and Mary that his humanity learned the sacrificial love calling him and all of humanity to be the recipients of God's gifts of incarnation and resurrection.

Anything lifted out of context becomes error when its appearance in isolation conflicts with the "truth" from which it has been lifted. Each year, the feast of Holy Family invites us to see the whole picture of family life's freely given obedience to the love of Jesus, Mary, and Joseph. No family member is exempt from "submission" because no family member is exempt from sharing in the love all are called to witness. God is love, and they who abide in love abide in God, and God in them (1 John 4:16).

QUESTIONS FOR YOUR REFLECTION

1. The dictionary defines "submission" as the act of submitting to the power of another. When one submits to the power of Christ's love, to what is one submitting? What is the submission asked of fathers in their headship of family life?

2. Why does St. Paul assign to fathers the first responsibility of witnessing Christ's love?

3. When husbands are charged with the responsibility of sacrificial love, what is the nature of the sacrifice? Without exception, what is the priority of sacrificial love?

4. How is St. Paul's use of the word "submissive" misunderstood when it is taken outside the context of Christ's sacrificial love for his Church?

The Christmas That Isn't What Christmas Was

WORD

Love was Stephen's weapon by which he gained every battle, and so won the crown signified by his name (St. Fulgentius of Ruspe, bishop).[4]

REFLECTION

While Christmas was a happy experience in our home, my mother rarely failed to sigh each year, "Christmas no longer seems to be Christmas." Her remark puzzled me. Later in life, I began to see that her lament sprang from a childhood approach to Christmas that seeks to be transformed into an adult experience of its fullest joy. It is for that experience that the Church celebrates the martyrdom of St. Stephen the day after Christmas. She invites our understanding of suffering as an indispensable dimension of Christ's incarnation.

My mother's lament was evidence of a one-dimension perspective of Christmas. As a child, she undoubtedly focused only on the birth of the child Jesus on a day two thousand years ago. That perspective of Christ's incarnation was, and still is, valuable. But her lament raises the interesting question, Is the birth of Jesus in Bethlehem two thousand years ago all there is to Christmas for the adult mind?

The feast of St. Stephen's martyrdom is the Church's assertion that a Christmas season without the dimension of Christ's paschal mystery is not adequate for an adult appreciation of Christ's incarnation. Christmas will never be what it was in our childhood because that isn't what Christmas fully is in our adulthood. The fullness of Christmas' joy springs from the pangs of pain that accompany every birth. Parents of newborn children experience indescribable joy in the face of births indescribably painful.

The proximity of St. Stephen's martyrdom to the celebration of Christ's birth vividly expresses the beautiful truth that love transforms death into birth. With the eyes of faith and hope, St. Stephen peered into the endless depths of God's love longing to be revealed for the embrace of all. When faith enabled Stephen to see God's love for all men and women, his sentiments surely echoed God's:

> The heavens are my throne,
>> the earth is my footstool.
> What kind of house can you build for me;
>> what is to be my resting place? (Isa 66:1).

In her Christmas liturgy, the Church begs us not to lose sight of Christmas' roots in the soil of Christ's paschal mystery. Stephen's martyrdom invites us to peer into the very depths of the love that pierces this world's boundaries. Stephen was a witness of the love that Christ personified by his birth, death, and resurrection. Because of love, he emptied himself of God's heavenly companionship so that he might be born into companionship with our humanity (see Phil 2:6-7). After thirty-three years of earthly existence, Jesus died on the cross so that his resurrection from the dead might be the witness of God's indescribable love ready to be born in humankind.

When Christmas is merely a recess from our crosses, we refuse to hand over to God the "womb" where Christ might be born again in our lives. Our crosses are imperative if joy is to be the fruit of Christmas' celebration. When Christ clothed himself with our humanity, he also clothed himself with our way of the cross. Christmas becomes ever more joyful when we invite Christ to share our sufferings, for they are the wombs of his birth *today*.

Is it really true that the shepherds who saw Jesus in the manger and touched his earthly body were more fortunate than we? A resounding NO! We who live two thousand years away from Christ's historical birthplace are far closer to Christ's birth from the crosses of our lives today. Our sufferings are the pangs of his real presence through us, with us, and in us, *now*!

Christmas is not a holiday away from suffering. It is ray of God's Son, who celebrated the paschal mystery of death and resurrection. December 25 celebrates every day as a "little Easter" when daily we embrace our sufferings in exchange for the joy of Christ's risen presence within us. The gift of God's love enables us to cherish suffering as the infallible sign of Christ's hidden presence seeking birth from our crosses.

But more than that, God's love enables us to cherish our sufferings as infallible signs of our identity sealed with the identity of Christ. Jesus welcomed our humanity as his own so that his strength, his peace, and his joy might also be our own. That marvelous exchange of natures is the "amazing grace" of God's love, which no suffering can extinguish.

"Christmas no longer seems to be Christmas"? Not if its companion is the paschal mystery!

QUESTIONS FOR YOUR REFLECTION

1. Why does the liturgy beckon us to reflect on the martyrdom of St. Stephen the day after Christmas?

2. In what respect does the transforming power of Christ's incarnation leave us untouched when we focus *only* on the birth of Jesus?

3. The word "martyr" means "witness." In what way is St. Stephen's martyrdom a witness of Christ's ongoing incarnation throughout time? What is St. Stephen's witness saying to us in this Christmas season?

4. How does the inclusion of our sufferings with the joys of Christ's incarnation give another view to St. Leo's words, "Today our Savior *is* born to us" (italics mine)?[5]

The Bay Isn't the Whole Ocean

WORD

This is what we proclaim to you:
what was from the beginning,
what we have heard,
what we have seen with our eyes,
what we have looked upon
and our hands have touched—
we speak of the word of life (1 John 1:1).

REFLECTION

A small boy's only view of the world had been the boundaries of a bay near his home. Almost every day he and his father spent a large part of their time fishing in that bay. One fishless day, the father said to his son, "Let's head for the ocean."

Puzzled, the boy asked, "Isn't this the ocean?" Grinning, the father replied: "Son, the bay we can see is only a part of the ocean we can't see. Our bay here at home isn't the whole ocean!"

This story touches on the heart of St. John the Evangelist's message, "We speak of the word of life." Unlike the other three evangelists, Matthew, Mark, and Luke, John's writings say little about the earthly identity of Jesus. His mission calls us to go beyond the "bay" of Christ's own human life here upon earth to the "ocean" of divine life, from whence he came and which he has called us to share.

The celebration of St. John the Evangelist's feast day soon after Christmas invites us to focus on his "ocean" view of Christ's incarnation, far beyond Bethlehem's "bay" view. His larger meaning of incarnation takes us far beyond the historical meaning easily grasped by human experience and imagination.

St. John's writings inspire us to expand our vision of Christ's incarnation beyond what we can see and touch. Yes, he heard, saw, and touched the earthly presence of Christ's eternal identity. But his touch of Christ's physical presence did not bring him the joy yet to be revealed from the depths of Christ's hiddenness. For John, then, the full power of God's Word was not confined to his physical presence. He wanted to proclaim the good news that God's Word had been raised from all earthly limitations to become the power and the presence of God for all men and women until the end of time.

St. Augustine asks an important question for all who have lived since the time of Christ's earthly presence: "Are we less favored than those who both saw and heard [Christ's physical presence]?" He replies, "We have fellowship with [Christ's disciples], because we and they share the same faith. . . . 'And our fellowship is with God the Father and Jesus Christ his Son. . . . We write this to you to make your joy complete'—complete in that fellowship, in that love and in that unity" (St. Augustine, bishop).[6]

When Christ received his humanity from Mary, he clothed himself with all of humanity so that all men and women might be marked with his own divine identity. St. John begins his gospel, "In the beginning was the Word, and the Word was with God" (John 1:1). The Word became flesh so that all men and women might touch the presence of God's Word and be transformed.

Are we who live today less favored than those who heard, saw, and touched the physical presence of Jesus? We are *more* favored! With the coming of the Holy Spirit after Christ's ascension, God's Word became flesh in us, to embrace us with the love of his transforming intimacy. In our oneness with Christ we have been raised to the heights of God's identity. The presence of God's Word, no longer confined to Christ's physical presence, has touched all of humankind to transform us into the family of God. "See what love the Father has bestowed on us," St. John writes, "in letting us be called children of God" (1 John 3:1).

How fruitless, then, are those longings to return to Christ's Bethlehem manger. Is the risen Christ less present to us today than he was in Bethlehem? He is not! God's Word dwells deeply within those "who believe in his name [and] who [are] begotten not by blood, nor by carnal desire, nor by [humankind's] willing it, but by God" (John 1:12-13). Far more fruitful is the longing to embrace the Word now, so that God might embrace and transform our hearts.

To keep God's Word confined to the "bay" of our Christmas nostalgia for Bethlehem's crèche is to be untouched by God's transforming Word in the "ocean" of his presence all around us. None of us touch the real presence of God in the bay of our Christmas nostalgia unless we realize that God's Word reaches out to touch us, *today*, from the ocean of his love.

QUESTIONS FOR YOUR REFLECTION

1. St. John writes "The Word became flesh" (John 1:14). In what way does the Word of God continue to become flesh today?

2. In what sense is the popular view of Christmas a "bay" view of Christ's incarnation? What is the "ocean" view we may be missing?

3. In the light of Christ's birth in the poverty of a barren cave, where can we expect to find Christ waiting to be born in our midst?

4. The shepherds touched the physical presence of God's Word. How, then, can we justify St. Augustine's assertion that we who live today touch the Word of God more intimately than those who saw him in Bethlehem two thousand years ago?

DECEMBER 28
HOLY INNOCENTS, MARTYRS

How Many Divisions Did Jesus Command?

WORD

[Herod], your throne is threatened by the source of grace— so small, yet so great—who is lying in the manger (St. Quodvultdeus, bishop).[7]

REFLECTION

While speaking derisively of the Pope, Josef Stalin sneered, "The Pope! How many divisions has *he* got?"[8] Many years later, one of Stalin's Soviet successors, Mikhail Gorbachev, stunned by the uprising of countless "divisions" of men and women crying out in behalf of human dignity, sat down in the peaceful surroundings of the Pope's presence to discuss matters of justice and peace.

Josef Stalin attacked the vicar of Christ, whose earthly office does not command "divisions" of earthly power. He mocked an office that represents the power of God's Word dwelling within us. That power first appeared as a tiny child in a manger and has never ceased inspiring countless "divisions" of men and women, whose human dignity was the child's reason for coming. St. Quodvultdeus writes: "A tiny child is born, who is a great king. Wise men are led to him from afar. They come to adore one who lies in a manger and yet reigns in heaven and on earth."[9]

How interesting that when rulers violate the dignity of the defenseless "divisions," they unwittingly open the door to the power of God, who unfailingly restores goodness where once fear reigned! Speaking of King Herod, whose own fear of the infant king moved him to decree the deaths of all newborn male infants, St. Quodvultdeus speaks as if to Herod: "[God] is using you, all unaware of it, to work out his own purposes freeing souls from captivity to the devil. . . . While you vent your fury against the child, you are already paying him homage, and do not know it."[10]

To this very day, the martyrdom of the Holy Innocents remains to answer those who sneer, "How many divisions has Christ got?" To which St. Quodvultdeus responds: "To what merits of their own do the [Holy Innocents] owe this kind of victory? They cannot speak, yet they bear witness to Christ. They cannot use their limbs to engage in battle, yet already they bear off the palm of victory."[11]

These holy infants will always remain silent witnesses to the futility of a security that employs the "peacemaking" instruments of war and destruction. The silence and defenselessness of these innocent martyrs have kept open the door through which the peace of Christ the King never ceases to reveal his justice in behalf of human dignity. This peace possesses a power that is real, effective, and lasting. St. Paul writes: "Neither death nor life, neither angels nor principalities, neither the present nor the future, nor powers, neither height nor depth nor any other creature, will be able to separate us from the love of God that comes to us in Christ Jesus, our Lord" (Rom 8:38-39).

On this side of eternity, it is impossible for us to penetrate the depths of God's eternal concerns. But we know one thing: "God is love" (1 John 4:8). Throughout this vast universe, only God's creature who bears the image of God's divinity also bears the worth of God's concern. Human life possesses the dignity of being not only the garment of Christ's incarnation but also the temple of God's Spirit, whose burning love for humanity countless divisions of power cannot conquer. At no time is the power of God's love more evident than when the whole universe, without weapons of destruction, cries out for justice and peace.

When Pope John Paul II journeyed twice to his native Poland, he came not with divisions of troops but with the simple message of God's burning love for the countless "divisions" of people who have longed to bask once again in the light and the warmth of that love. His voice of hope, echoing the voices of the "tiny child . . . in a manger" and the Holy Innocents, ignited the roaring fire of joy no wall could withstand.

"The Pope! How many divisions has *he* got?" None, was the Pope's reply, none save the Holy Innocents, whose only weapon was their silent witness still proclaiming the victory of God's love in the hearts of defenseless millions. "How great a gift of grace is here! To what merits of their own do the [Holy Innocents] owe this kind of victory? They cannot speak, yet they bear witness to Christ. They cannot use their limbs to engage in battle, yet already they bear off the palm of victory."[12]

QUESTIONS FOR YOUR REFLECTION

1. Toward the end of 1989, the free world was stunned by the lightning speed with which nearly all of Eastern Europe showed signs that the foundations of Communism were crumbling. How are these "signs of the times" evidence of God's presence among millions of "innocents"?

2. St. Paul writes, "When I am powerless, it is then that I am strong" (2 Cor 12:10). When Josef Stalin sneered, "The Pope! How many

divisions has *he* got?" how did he underestimate the power of the papacy?

3. For two thousand years, the Holy Innocents have been remembered. How would you respond to St. Quodvultdeus' question, "To what merits of their own do the [Holy Innocents] owe this kind of victory"? What was the weakness that became their strength?

4. It is fear that causes nations to spend billions on "weapons of strength." What is the fear, masked by "divisions" of troops, that allegedly keeps the peace?

DECEMBER 29
FIFTH DAY IN THE OCTAVE OF CHRISTMAS

Not What You Say but What I Saw

WORD

Before the Son of God became man his goodness was hidden, for God's mercy is eternal, but how could such goodness be recognized? . . . God's Son came in the flesh so that mortal man could see and recognize God's kindness (St. Bernard, abbot).[13]

REFLECTION

One morning before sunup a hospital staff-person called my attention to a young man of eighteen who had been seriously injured in an automobile accident. As I approached his bedside in the hospital emergency room, I saw my own self thirty-six years before, lying in the same condition from an accident that took the life of another person. Identifying myself with this young man was not a new experience, for often I had relived that terrible November night in my eighteenth year.

After I had anointed the young man, he asked me if I would visit him again. I promised that I would. His insistence that I return intrigued me.

Two days later I found him greatly improved and in good spirits. As we visited, he surprised me when suddenly he asked, "You were once in a car wreck, weren't you?"

"How did you know that?" I asked.

"Well," he replied, "you were the only one in the emergency room who knew what I was feeling. It wasn't what you said; it was what I saw."

Because of the young man's insight, my conviction that human experiences can become indelibly stamped on our identities was confirmed. Experiences reveal themselves in our actions, even though we are not conscious of their impact. My visit with the young man led me to appreciate the transforming power that God's Word offers to our identities. I reasoned that if an automobile accident could forever mark my identity, how much more could God's Word mark it with the identity of Christ.

To the Colossians St. Paul writes: "You heard of [God's message of] hope . . . which has come to you, has borne fruit, and has continued to grow in your midst. . . . By the might of [God's] glory you will be endowed with the strength needed to stand fast, even to endure joyfully whatever may come . . ." (Col 1:5-6, 11).

The incarnation is a message of hope. It provides us with the certainty that within the context of our humanity, God is revealed *now*! This mystery of faith is not confined to a doctrinal formulation destined only for our heads. It is a way of *being* whereby the identity of Christ is unmistakably revealed in our hearts. The Son of God, though without falling into sin, vested himself with our fallen humanity. Christ embraced our sinful nature with the infallible promise that his transforming presence would restore us to the image and likeness of God.

Before the coming of Christ, humankind lived its relationship with God *only* by way of promise. When the Son of God came in the flesh, he enabled all men and women to live in relationship with God by way of faith's experience of God. This experience is not our feelings; rather, our experience of Christ's incarnation is Christ's own experience of his identity in ours. It bears repeating that the incarnation is more than a doctrinal formulation; it is the very identity of

Christ carved into our humanity, enabling all of us to radiate Christ's loving presence among all we find in our midst.

St. Bernard writes: "The fullness of time brought with it the fullness of divinity. God's Son came in the flesh so that mortal men [and women] could see and recognize God's kindness. When God reveals his humanity, his goodness cannot possibly remain hidden. To show his kindness what more could he do beyond taking my human form? . . . How could he have shown more clearly than by taking on himself our condition?"[14]

The young man to whom I ministered saw no visible evidences of my own experience of an automobile accident. With the eyes of human faith, however, he saw the fruits of my otherwise tragic accident experience. Without my realizing it, the experience of an accident had transformed my identity, enabling me to share the fruits of that experience—understanding, compassion, gentleness, forgiveness, and a sense of hope that summoned him to look beyond his suffering.

The mystery of Christ's incarnation bids us to rely on God's gifts of faith and hope, so that from our sufferings we too might experience the rebirth of life. We believe that Christ's presence will be indelibly stamped on our identities and that our own lives will become sacraments of Christ's love for those who long for his touch. Those whose lives we have touched will surely say, "It wasn't what you said; it was what I saw."

QUESTIONS FOR YOUR REFLECTION

1. Since feelings are integral components of human identity, why are they not guarantees of authentic experiences of Christ? How do human feelings sometimes thwart faith's power to give birth to Christ's identity in ours?

2. Why do the effects of faith in us more often than not surprise us when their witness is clearly seen by others?

3. Can you recall your own surprise when another person spoke movingly of your Christlike impact on him or her? Why were you surprised? What is the difference between felt experiences of Christ and faith experiences of Christ?

4. What is the basic difference between the faith of those who lived before Christ and the faith of those who have lived after Christ?

This Too Will Pass

WORD

The saying, "Know yourself," means . . . that we should recognize and acknowledge in ourselves the God who made us in his own image, for if we do this, we in turn will be recognized and acknowledged by our maker. So let us not be at enmity with ourselves, but change our way of life without delay (St. Hippolytus, priest).[15]

REFLECTION

In an issue of *Markings* I began with this story:

A wealthy man lost track of all he possessed. Never completely happy, he earnestly believed that more wealth would silence the hunger for a contentment he longed to experience in his life.

It came to his attention that somewhere on a mountaintop there lived a very wise man whose one and only four-word utterance pointed the way to ultimate happiness. The desire to find this wise man consumed the richest of all men and women.

Immediately he commissioned teams of searchers to scale all the mountains throughout the world that he might learn the way to perfect happiness. As the years went by and his riches dwindled, the rich man's hope never once abated. At last, one of the teams found the old man. With his money supply now exhausted, the once wealthy searcher for the old man's wisdom was brought to the mountaintop where he stood in the presence of his quest for happiness.

"O wise one," he began, "give me the four words which can bring me the riches of this world's richest happiness."

After a few moments, the old man gazed beyond the pinnacle of his mountaintop habitat, stretched out his arms as if to embrace the whole world, and sighed:

"This too will pass!"[16]

This is really everyone's story. Without exception, we spend our lives seeking meaning in every nook and cranny of our lives. Like the man in search of more riches, we too search for the riches of human identity. The moment will present itself for us to decide what we perceive to be valuable for our identity. In reality there are but two choices: We must choose either this world's meaning of human existence or faith's meaning of what lies beyond the boundaries of this world. Whatever we choose as life's centerpiece will become our identity. Why? Because, as Walter Cronkite put it, "That's the way it is." God created us in such a way that whatever we choose as absolutely central will form our identity.

St. Hippolytus writes: "The saying, 'Know yourself' means . . . that we should recognize and acknowledge in ourselves the God who made us in his own image."

To know anything means to acknowledge *why* it exists. If, for example, a name does not shed light on what it stands for, we ask, "What's it for?" In other words, we define any reality by how it affects and forms our lives. If we have decided that this world's goods are the ultimate reason for our existence, then a very shallow "faith" will lead us to the illusion that the acquisition of as many of this world's goods as possible is ultimate happiness. The gullibility that poses as faith, alas, is delusion, and the deluded discover that "this too will pass!"

The Son of God became one of us that he might proclaim the alternative choice for human definition. His humanity enabled the power of his Word to answer the question, What's humanity for? Jesus addressed that question in the opening words of his public ministry: "Reform your lives! The kingdom of heaven is at hand" (Matt 4:17).

Inviting his listeners to look beyond this world's perishables as central to human meaning, he offered a meaning of human life that enables faith to be the re-forming instrument of human identity's imperishable destiny. "Our faith," writes St. Hippolytus, "is not founded on empty words; nor are we carried away by mere caprice or beguiled by specious arguments. [Rather], we put our faith in words spoken by the power of God, spoken by the Word himself at God's command."[17]

The wise man's four-word formula for happiness, "this too will pass," brought the visitor to the end of his "faith." Not so with those who believe the Word of God. The birth of Christ enabled God to reach out with a one-word message for a happiness that this world, without Christ, cannot surmise. God's Word is Jesus. This is the Word about whom St. Paul writes to the Colossians: "[Christ Jesus] is the image of the invisible God, the first-born of all creatures. In him everything in heaven and on earth was created, things visible and invisible. . . . In him everything continues in being" (Col 1:15-17).

The presence of Jesus, then, is the center, the meaning, and the *only* reason for our identity. It is of our centerpiece, then, that Jesus pleads, "Reform your lives."

This will *not* pass!

QUESTIONS FOR YOUR REFLECTION

1. "This too will pass" are not, of themselves, words of indictment against the possession of this world's goods. To what extent, however, are they an indictment against the reason for the rich man's pursuit of happiness?

2. In what way is faith in this world's perishables as sources of perfect happiness a perversion of our capacity to believe? What is the tragedy of making this world's goods the centerpiece of life's meaning?

3. Why is it imperative for us to know, that is, to experience, Jesus Christ in order for us to know ourselves?

4. The word "reform" is often interpreted as a call to desist from evil ways. How does the word spelled "re-form" deepen its meaning? How does it affect identity?

Christ's Nativity Never Ceases

WORD

In Christ the fullness of deity resides in bodily form. Yours is a share of his fullness, in him who is the head of every principality and power (Col 2:9-10).

REFLECTION

During my first two years of college, I worked for room and board at a funeral home where I enjoyed the company of its director, Dan Boone. Dan's reputation was that of a "nice guy." Low key, pleasant, and oh so bland, his interests seemed confined to chitchat about work, sports, and speculations about United States involvement in a threatening war.

I thought I had Dan fairly well sized up, felt comfortable working with him, and rated him little more than a passing figure in my here-today-gone-tomorrow world. Little did I suspect that a new Dan Boone was about to be born before my eyes.

That birth took place shortly before the college prom. Knowing that I had no car with which to escort my date, Dan Boone offered his car, with himself as chauffeur. Elated and speechless, I gladly accepted. However, despite his delightful largesse, Dan Boone was still the "nice guy" I thought I knew.

Early in the evening of the prom, he arrived at my apartment, ready to be of service. He found me and my own brother Dan harmonizing some of the "good old songs." As he strolled into our company, he suddenly broke into song with a deep, rich baritone. From the depths of his hiddenness, the Dan Boone I knew gave birth to a Dan Boone I had never met. By way of his gifted voice, my perception of his personhood was forever changed. In the harmony of that moment, a new Dan Boone arrived in my life.

I entered the seminary several months later, and I never saw Dan Boone again. Nevertheless, this man whose hiddenness had become a reality fifty years ago has never left me. From the rich experience of discovering a Dan Boone I did not know, I have found myself inclined to expect from others a richness of personhood that faith and hope insist lies hidden in everyone's mystery. My experience with the new Dan Boone has often cautioned me not to settle on fixed first perceptions of others. These become unjust judgments because they hold hostage the hidden features of personhood longing for liberation. It goes without saying that the greatest gift we give others is our conviction that they are more than what we might surmise.

Herein lies an insight into the mystery of Christ's nativity. His giftedness extends far beyond the human birth he experienced one day two thousand years ago. The precise day of his birth is not the primary reason for our yearly celebration of Christmas. We celebrate the nativity of Christ because he *continues* to be born deep within the mystery of our lives *today!* Each of us offers God's Holy Spirit the opportunity to bring forth Christ's birth from the hidden depths of our gifts. Each Christmas, God's Spirit asks for more than mere recollection of his historical birth as we gather to celebrate Christmas. The Holy Spirit invites us to embrace our sacred potential of being Christ's continuing incarnation throughout time.

The birth of Christ's real presence within us is likewise *our rebirth.* Christ came into this world not to be a conversation piece. He embraced all of humanity's potential for its transformation into the new persons God created us to become. St. Paul says it this way: "In Christ the fullness of deity resides in bodily form. Yours is a share of his fullness, in him who is the head of every principality and power." Indeed, each of us not only shares in God's fullness but we share to the extent that God's fullness might be made visible in the uniqueness of our lives. The appearance of Christ's newness, revealed in our uniqueness, transforms us and lets us embrace more deeply the Christened persons we little dream we are.

In a Christmas sermon, St. Leo the Great exclaims: "Every believer regenerated in Christ, no matter in what part of the whole world he [or she] may be, breaks with that ancient way of life that derives from original sin, and by rebirth is transformed into a new [person]. Henceforth [all are] reckoned to be of the stock, not of [an] earthly father, but of Christ, who became Son of Man precisely that [all] could become [children] of God; for unless he had come down to us, none of us by our own merits could ever go up to him" (St. Leo the Great, pope).[18]

When Dan Boone's beautiful voice enhanced our harmony, he gave birth to a newness of his personhood we hardly suspected. His newness also became ours. And so it is with Christ. He came into the world to call all of us away from the dissonance of this world's "harmony" so that we might forever share the harmony of Christ's own Trinitarian life. He came to announce that this world's image does not harmonize with who we *really* are. "Therefore," St. Leo prays, "may those 'who were born, not of blood nor of the will of the flesh nor of the will of [humankind], but of God' offer to the Father their harmony as [humanity] joined in peace."[19]

QUESTIONS FOR YOUR REFLECTION

1. Why are fixed perceptions among parents and children detrimental to the health and happiness of families? among parishes? among associations of workers?

2. In what way do the virtues of faith, humility, and patience enable us to call forth from others hidden dimensions of their personhood? Name other virtues you deem necessary for the birth of hidden personhood.

3. Why is a deeper knowledge of ourselves vitally important to God? How is our uniqueness an instrument of Christ's ongoing birth toward the fullness in time?

4. In what way is Christmas more than a commemoration of Christ's historical birth? Other than the buying of gifts, what does Christmas mean to you? Do you think that Christmas' annual binge of buying excuses us from not facing this question?

The Marvelous Exchange

WORD

It was fitting that when bringing many [children] to glory, God, for whom and through whom all things exist, should make their leader in the work of salvation perfect through suffering. He who consecrates and those who are consecrated have one and the same Father. Therefore he is not ashamed to call them brothers [and sisters], saying, "I will announce your name to my brothers [and sisters]. . . . Here am I, and the children God has given me!" (Heb 2:10-12, 13).

REFLECTION

In his book *Mary at the Foot of the Cross,* James Cardinal Hickey writes about Fr. Karl Rahner's reply when he was asked about the declining devotion to Mary. "All Christians, Catholics and Protestants alike, face the common temptation of turning the central truths of the Faith into abstractions, 'and abstractions have no need of mothers' "[20]

Throughout the octave of Christmas, the Liturgy of the Hours invites us to be in touch not with the abstraction of incarnation but with the birth of God's Son, born of Mary and clothed with our humanity. It is not unimportant that the Church climaxes eight days of Christmas reflection with Mary's motherhood of Jesus as central to the wider and deeper meaning of incarnation. The motherhood of Mary is not an abstraction meant only for storage in the mind. Mary gave birth both to the person of Jesus and to the fullest possible meaning of human purpose and existence.

Consider this implication: Our humanity has been graced through Mary's motherhood to share a communion with God's life as intimately as Christ shared communion with human life. The communion that exists between Christ's divinity and our humanity is like the communion shared by Jesus and his Father. Little wonder, then, that at Evening Prayer before the feast of Mary's motherhood, all who pray the Liturgy of the Hours cry out in wonderment: "O marvelous exchange! [Humankind's] Creator has become man, born of a virgin. We have been made sharers in the divinity of Christ who humbled himself to share in our humanity" (antiphon 1, Evening Prayer I).[21]

This "marvelous exchange" is not an abstraction meant for mental gymnastics. Mary literally gave to God's Son not only her own sinless humanity but also the potential for all of humanity to be sinless. That's because her sinlessness qualified her to possess human integrity and to endow all of humanity with that integrity. When Mary gave human existence to Jesus, she gave birth to the hallmark of our existence. Christ's sinlessness enabled him to accept Mary's integrity and to pass it on to us.

St. Athanasius offers this insight concerning the motherhood of Mary: "Gabriel used careful and prudent language when he announced [the birth of Jesus]. He did not speak of 'what will be born *in you*' to avoid the impression that a body would be introduced into the womb from outside; he spoke of 'what will be born *from you*' so that we might know by faith that a child originated within her and from her" (St. Athanasius, bishop).[22]

Mary's motherhood initiated the "marvelous exchange" of divinity and humanity. It verified the purpose of human existence. As surely as Mary gave to Jesus the integrity of humanity, so she enabled God to restore humanity to God's original plan of being in the likeness of God. Cardinal Hickey reflects, "We are called to bear witness not to something—some abstraction—whether it be called Redemption, liberation, or affirmation; we are sent to be witnesses of Someone—whom we call 'Son of God' and 'Son of Mary.' "[23]

Mary did not give birth to an abstraction called "incarnation." She gave birth to "Someone," whom she bore in her womb. Mary gave to the "Someone" of God's human personhood the vesture of both her humanity and ours. Jesus' birth *from* Mary gave him the "way" for our rescue from the separation from communion with God. His "way" has also become our "way" to live in communion with God.

When faith lacks "Someone" to still restless hearts, devotion is in danger. On the final day of the octave of Christmas, the Church offers us the Mother of God, who begs us to embrace her Son rather than abstractions—either *about* her or her Son. Her presence at the juncture of the Christmas and Epiphany seasons begs us also to be the juncture of God's divinity and our humanity. Only when our own hearts become the motherhood of Mary *today* will we experience the reappearance of devotion to Mary from a humanity whose motherhood of Jesus, hidden in both men and women, longs for devotion.

QUESTIONS FOR YOUR REFLECTION

1. Why is faith in an abstraction about Mary's motherhood of Jesus an escape from the implications of Christ's incarnation? What is the difference between faith in an abstraction *about* Christ and faith *in* Christ, who is "Someone"?

2. In the light of the "marvelous exchange" between God's divinity and our humanity, why is it imperative that we receive the truths of our faith into our hearts rather than keep them in our heads? What difference does it make where these truths reside, as long as we give them our assent?

3. What is the difference between assent and consent?

4. As far as we are personally concerned, how does Mary's motherhood of Jesus concern us? What does our responsibility become when Christ's birth *from* Mary is applied to us?

One Note Doesn't Make
the Whole Song

WORD

*In the gifts that [the Spirit] distributes we can see the Spirit
as a whole in relation to its parts. We are all members
of one another, but with different gifts according to the
grace God gives us* (St. Basil the Great, bishop).[24]

REFLECTION

At the tender age of eight, I began to be fascinated by our family piano. I was intrigued with its unlimited possibilities, which daily invited me to explore new vistas of beauty. Day after day the piano's thirteen-note scales tempted my touch to bring to birth lovely songs from their diversity.

The imperative of each note being utterly different from each other note raised a question in my mind. Could there be harmony without diversity? When I asked my father how the piano would sound if all the keys were tuned in the key of C, he dryly observed, "Well, one note doesn't make the whole song."

Years later, as I studied theology, my father's remark enabled me to resolve at least some of my difficulties concerning the Holy Spirit's role in our lives. As I wrestled with doctrinal formulations about God's Spirit, I pictured myself at a piano, with its marvel of diversity awaiting my gift of bringing diversity together in the marvel of harmony. Experience at the piano made it clear that just as its artistry creates the harmony of a song from the diversity of sounds, so the artistry of God's Spirit calls forth from humankind's panorama of diversity the marvel of God's many-splendored harmony.

Long before St. Basil made his appearance in my world of theological reflection, I had learned from the piano what his wisdom later confirmed. From his own theological reflections on the Holy Spirit, he observes that from our diversity of gifts, God's overshadowing Spirit gives birth to the oneness of humankind in the likeness of God's Trinitarian communion. "In the gifts that he distributes," he writes, "we can see the Spirit as a whole in relation to its parts. We are all members of one another, but with different gifts according to the grace God gives us."

It seems to me that a sign of the Holy Spirit's active presence in our lives is the ease with which we relate to diversity. Those who are at ease amidst diversity have listened to the Spirit's call to fix their eyes on Christ. The body of Christ here on earth is the diversity in which God's Spirit longs to form the harmony of God's presence. God's Spirit sees each of us in terms of the wholeness we were created to mirror.

Very often diversity is feared, because those who see truth's wholeness only in their one note of truth are threatened by the immense scale of truths they are invited to embrace with the gift of faith. It is in the face of their dis-ease with diversity that they cry out, "Division!" Diversity is not synonymous with division. Division arises only when one of diversity's parts is perceived as the whole of reality. Each part of diversity is a part of the truth, not the whole truth.

St. John's story of the Samaritan woman (see John 4:4-26) is a good example of one who, until Jesus challenged her to worship "in spirit and in truth," had seen the wholeness of truth only from her point of view. St. Basil writes: "As the Father is seen in the Son, so the Son is seen in the Spirit. To worship in the Spirit, then, is to have our minds open to the light, as we may learn from our Lord's words to the Samaritan woman. Misled by the tradition of her country, she imagined that it was necessary to worship in a certain place, but our Lord gave her a different teaching. He told her that one must worship in Spirit and in truth, and clearly by the truth he meant himself."[25]

Jesus is God's "new song," and we are the marvelous diversity of notes in whose harmony the wholeness of that song's beauty can be heard. Our happiness in this world is ours only to the extent that we see ourselves as an integral *part* of that song. Unhappiness becomes our lot when we see our part of the song as the whole song.

Christmas' truth lovingly hands us on to Epiphany's truth. We are asked to gaze "in Spirit and in truth" beyond Christ in the manger to Christ in the wholeness of his presence on earth as he is in heaven. This gaze is fixed on the Spirit's light drawing us to embrace the fullness of Christ, whose body is our communion both on earth and in heaven. This is the communion God's Spirit inspired St. Paul to write: "Since you have been raised up in company with Christ, set your heart on what pertains to higher realms where Christ is seated at God's right hand. Be intent on things above rather than on things of earth. After all, you have died! Your life is hidden now with Christ in God. When Christ our life appears, then you will appear with him in glory" (Col 3:1-4).

Thank God "one note doesn't make the whole song."

QUESTIONS FOR YOUR REFLECTION

1. Why does the Holy Spirit distribute a diversity of gifts among God's people for the achievement of unity? Isn't that a contradiction? Explain.

2. What is the difference between unity and uniformity? When uniformity is regarded as the ideal of Church unity, why will pride be its chief effect (see Col 2:20-23)?

3. *E pluribus unum* (from diversity comes unity) is the motto found on American coins. Although these words can also be applied to ecclesial unity, what is the difference between national unity and Church unity? What is the source of unity in each?

4. In the light of question 3, how are divisions between Church and state revealed, for example, in matters of race relations, "sanctity of private choice," "mercy" to the incurably sick, "justice" to criminals awaiting capital punishment, and the "peacemaking potential" to justify the storage of nuclear weaponry?

Interns Now but Saints Forever!

WORD

Love of God is the first to be commanded, but love of neighbor is the first to be put into practice (St. Augustine, bishop).[26]

REFLECTION

Two years after my ordination to the priesthood, I was assigned as chaplain at a moderately large hospital. The example of medical interns continues to be the most vivid memory of that four-year assignment. As I watched these dedicated men and women under the watchful eye of deeply concerned physicians, I envied the internship that was initiating them into the practice of medicine. I thought of the absence of a comparable internship initiating me into the practice of priesthood.

Had I begun the practice of medicine with an internship like the one with which I began the priesthood, I might have soon lost my license to be a physician. Since that time of regret over forty years ago, this situation has been attended to. Today, a kind of internship or "novitiate" for ministry is required of candidates for the priesthood, permanent diaconate, and religious life, under the watchful eyes of deeply concerned and dedicated pastoral workers.

I am grateful to the medical profession for the witness of an internship that enabled the interns to "pass over" from study to practice. Beyond its new perspective for the ministry, it has also opened my eyes to the much larger internship relative to human purpose for all men and women. The witness of guided pastoral care in preparation for professional expertise has guided me to examine the "internship" necessary for the practice of life in Christ and its relationship to our lives with one another.

It bears repeating: God did not create us to become experts in the ways of this world. Under God's watchful eye, we live in this world as interns toward the expertise of eternal life. We live *in,* not *of,* the world (see 1 John 4:5-6). Life in this world is an internship for eternal life. None of us can see the presence of Christ in this world as we see the world itself. Nevertheless, we have been given the eyes of faith to see Christ's hidden presence in the world. The capacity to "see" Christ's presence in our midst comes under God's watchful "eye" of faith as we practice our daily internship in the ways of faith.

In his "Treatise on John," St. Augustine does not use the word "internship" as he speaks of this world's purpose. Within the context of Christ's two commandments, love for God and neighbor, St. Augustine sketches the nature of our internship as we journey toward eternal life: "These two commandments must be always in your thoughts and in your hearts, treasured, acted on, fulfilled. Love of God is the first to be commanded, but the love of neighbor is the first to be put into practice. . . . Since you do not yet see God, you merit the vision of God by loving your neighbor. By loving your neighbor you prepare your eye to see God. St. John says clearly: 'If you do not love [others] whom you see, how will you love God whom you do not see?' "[27]

Love of God is God's first command because God is our final destiny. Yet, while we live in this world that final destiny can neither be seen nor experienced except by way of faith. Through faith we are beckoned by the love we cannot see to love those we can see. Paradoxically, then, God's second command must be our first concern. It is in our faithfulness to this second command that we obtain the fruits of God's first command. The love of neighbor is our "internship" for eternal life.

Centuries before St. Augustine, St. Paul wrote to the Colossians of their internship for the practice of eternal life. He exhorted them first to "put to death whatever in [their] nature is rooted in earth: fornication, uncleanness, passion, evil desires, and the lust which is idolatry" (Col 3:5). He then reminded them that the life of which they had divested themselves prepared them to be clothed in the likeness of God, whose Son Jesus clothed himself with our humanity. St. Paul does not leave us guessing about what the image of their life would be: "Because you are God's chosen ones, holy and beloved, clothe yourselves with heartfelt mercy, with kindness, humility, meekness, and patience. Bear with one another; forgive whatever grievances you have against one another. Forgive as the Lord has forgiven you. Over all these virtues put on love, which binds the rest together and makes them perfect" (Col 3:12-14).

Can we excuse ourselves from internship in the ways of God? Not at all! Christ refused to excuse himself from internship in the ways of humanity. Sin excepted, Christ embraced everything human so that he might be everything in all of us (see Col 3:11). He shared fully in our humanity that we might share fully in his divinity. This "marvelous exchange" is surely worth a lifetime of internship in the ways of God, as we "pass over" from this world's ways. Surely internship in time is well worth sainthood in eternity.

QUESTIONS FOR YOUR REFLECTION

1. Prescinding from the internships required for professional practice (medicine, law, ministry), what are other internships *all* of us are called to practice throughout our lifetimes? Why is the full-time quest for holiness by *all* of us not as quaint as some allege?

2. We are all created in the image and likeness of God. In the light of this basic human purpose, what does St. Paul mean when he writes, "Put to death whatever in your nature is rooted in earth" (Col 3:5)? What is our true rootedness and what is the internship required?

3. When the Son of God clothed himself with our human nature, he also clothed our humanity with God's divine nature. In the light of that "marvelous exchange," what is the internship to which we are all called in order to make that exchange our reality?

4. If the love of God is Christ's first commandment, why are we commanded to practice Christ's second commandment first? How does Christ's incarnation erase the suggestion of contradiction?

Look for Christ in Everything

WORD

Whatever you do, whether in speech or in action, do it in the name of the Lord Jesus. Give thanks to God the Father through him (Col 3:17).

REFLECTION

A childhood incident eventually led me to an understanding of Epiphany. It began one afternoon when I noticed a moderately large cardboard box lying in the street. "Hey!" I suggested to my companion, "Let's see if there's anything in that box." With nose wrinkled, he shrugged off my invitation with the quip, "It's only a box of nothing. . . . I ain't got time for nothing!" With that, he left me with a box of *his* "nothing."

I pondered my friend's assessment. Would I look like a scavenger if the neighbors saw me peering into a box of "nothing"? Happily, I rationalized that I said only, "Let's *see* if there's anything in that box." My hunch to see paid off. At my feet lay a box of the most "nothing" I had ever seen—a huge watermelon. With Herculean effort, I lifted it into my wagon and, like a conqueror, returned home past my friend's house, singing at the top of my voice, "I got plenty of nothing!"

This incident carved a large "something" on my young character. The neighbor boy's assessment of the box's "nothing" strongly suggested that I follow my hunches about the presence of "something" in everything. The incident gifted me with a keen sense of wonderment about nature's hidden treasures of goodness beyond the focus of our capacity to see with our eyes. This wonderment eventually led me to explore the mysteries of Christ's incarnation and epiphany inviting the Holy Spirit to manifest Christ's presence all around me.

43

In this connection, then, the time between Christmas and Epiphany is very important. In prayerful reflection the Church invites us to look beyond Bethlehem's manger to the manger of creation's manifestation of Christ's goodness and beauty. The Church gazes beyond the angelic light surrounding Christ's manger in Bethlehem and calls us to gaze at the epiphany of a star, a dove, and six stone jars filled with water. These "nothings" of nature are filled with the "somethings" of Christ's presence seeking to be revealed in our midst. St. Paul writes, "Whatever you do, whether in speech or in action, do it in the name of the Lord Jesus."

It has been estimated that St. Paul's "in Christ" and "in the name of the Lord" appear more than one hundred times in his letters. Life "in Christ" rests on the certainty that Christ dwells in all things. St. Paul's words to the Romans reflect this certainty: "Since the creation of the world, invisible realities, God's eternal power and divinity, have become visible, recognized through the things he has made" (Rom 1:20). In other words, the visible realities of this world are alive with the invisible presence of Christ, as they groan to deliver his presence from the hiddenness they embody. "Indeed," St. Paul writes, "We know that all creation groans and is in agony even until now" (Rom 8:19, 22).

St. Paul's deep respect for nature spills over into the writings of St. Maximus, who writes movingly of God's presence in nature: "Christ is God, for he has given all things their being out of nothing. Yet he is born as man by taking to himself our nature, flesh endowed with intelligent spirit. A star glitters by day in the East and leads the wise men to the place where the incarnate Word lies, to show that the Word, contained in the Law and the Prophets, surpasses in a mystical way knowledge derived from the senses, and to lead the Gentiles to the full light of knowledge" (St. Maximus the Confessor, abbot).[28]

How tragic that we settle for sense experience as the ultimate meaning of human life! In so doing we allow the presence of Christ to remain hidden in the womb of creation. We endow our five senses with a sovereignty that both defines and decides our ultimate worth. When we refuse to pass over from sense experience to faith and hope's manifestation of God's presence, we become slaves to the perishability that *without Christ* is this world's only worth.

"Epiphany" means "manifestation." Yes, creation "groans" to be the manifestation of God's hidden presence "in Christ." Epiphany means that the God who is invisible to the eyes of the body is visible to the eyes of faith. We live "in the name of the Lord Jesus" when it becomes our certainty that nothing of this world's goods, not even a star over Bethlehem, a dove, or six stone jars of water, lacks the presence of God. It bears repeating: "Whatever you do, whether in speech or in action, do it in the name of the Lord Jesus."

QUESTIONS FOR YOUR REFLECTION

1. Why is a healthy relationship with God endangered when the separation of sacred and secular is the basis of spiritual health?

2. More than one hundred times the term "in Christ" appears in the letters of St. Paul. What is the certainty evidenced in those who act "in Christ"?

3. Although Epiphany enjoys a very high ranking in the Church's hierarchy of liturgical celebrations, it receives little more than a glance from many worshipers. How is maturity of faith impeded when the historical birth of Jesus alone is the extent of devotion to Christ's incarnation? What does Epiphany's "manifestation" say about Christ's birth?

4. What is the difference between spirituality based on apparitions and spirituality based on the manifestation of Christ's presence in creation? Why is a preoccupation with Christmas, with hardly a glance at Epiphany, very often the reason for preoccupation with apparitions?

Longing: Count It a Priceless Possession

WORD

[God] has not yet given us the vision that will satisfy every desire; we have not yet drunk our fill of the fountain of life. So while all this remains in the future and we still walk by faith, absent from the Lord, while we still hunger and thirst for God's beauty, let us reverently celebrate the day he was born into our own servile condition (St. Augustine, bishop).[29]

REFLECTION

Although I was born and reared in the city, I looked forward to each summer's experience of working on a farm. Not the least of my blessings during those summers happened one hot day when the priceless gift of thirst held me hostage. Priceless gift? Let me explain.

I had been directed to cultivate a field of corn at the farthest end of the farm. On that terribly hot day I began my work in the worst possible way. Arriving with a horse-drawn cultivator, I discovered that I had left my thermos bottle of ice and water behind.

I felt trapped because there were no farms near the three-hundred-acre collage of crops and cattle where I worked. Although the sun promised more heat, I decided to "tough it out" until my return for lunch nearly five hours later.

The slow passage of time competed with the merciless sun, and water gradually became the sole focus of my attention. To this day I remember nothing about the first three hours of work except thirst. No other reality attracted my attention.

Late in the morning, I paused for shade under a tree. Despite my preoccupation with thirst, I could not help but notice the utter stillness all around me. Suddenly, I heard the sound of running water!

Not discounting the possibility of an auricular mirage, I walked toward the water's merciful sound until I stood over a partially broken underground tile, which had been laid for the removal of surplus water. I literally dropped, face down, over the exposed tile to drink of its pure and icy content. Savoring refreshment, I began to appreciate the priceless gift of thirst.

Long after that unforgettable experience, I came to appreciate deeply the priceless gift of longing for God's presence as a blessing from God. This longing unfolds as we suffer countless hungers, thirsts, in the poverty of deprivation. It also unfolds when, in the midst of plenty, we silence the longings for self-indulgence so that longings for God's presence might easily be discerned.

Whether we realize it or not, our deepest longing is for the imperishability of God's identity. Unfortunately, that longing remains hidden as long as we focus solely on perishability's demands for attention. These demands never cease as long as we pay them our heed. In so doing, the priceless gift of longing for the gift of transformation into God's image and likeness is kept hostage.

It does not go unnoticed either by St. Paul or St. Augustine that the birth of Jesus was also the birth of *his* human longing for God, from whom "he emptied himself and took the form of a slave, being born in the likeness of men" (Phil 2:7). St. Augustine adds: "What [person] knows all the treasures of wisdom and knowledge hidden in Christ, concealed in the poverty of his flesh? Scripture says 'Although he was rich he became poor for our sake to enrich us by his poverty.' "[30]

Christ emptied himself of equality with his Father so that he might humanly experience "in the poverty of his flesh" the longing that had been the hunger and thirst of all humanity. He experienced longing for God so that we might attend to our mutual longing, oneness with God and one another, humanity's first vocation.

A frequent complaint laments that God delays answering our prayers. Yet God's "delay" is really Christ's mission of experiencing *his* longing in *our* deepest longings for union with God. God delays answering our prayers for lesser thirsts so that the door of our inner being might be opened for Christ to dwell within the greater thirsts of our longing for God. God's delays become the unquenchable thirsts for union with God, who is the refreshing reality of our lives.

How beautifully St. Paul frames this thought: "Pray perseveringly, be attentive to prayer, and pray in a spirit of thanksgiving. Pray for us, too, that God may provide us with an opening to proclaim the mystery of Christ, for which I am a prisoner. Pray that I may speak it clearly, as I must" (Col 4:2-4).

It is in "the poverty of [our] flesh," then, that Christ manifests humankind's longings to be like God. Our lesser longings become priceless when Christ's "marvelous exchange" of divinity for humanity links our lesser and greater longings in the likeness of God's image.

QUESTIONS FOR YOUR REFLECTION

1. In what way might technology and its promise of "instant" living prevent the voice of longing for God from gaining our attention?

2. How does God's "delay" in answering our prayers school us in the "art" of longing for God?

3. When one displays bitterness toward God for not answering prayer, by what purpose of human existence has one probably defined his or her life?

4. Why did Christ want to live our experience of longing for God? How does this longing in his life affect our lives?

FROM JANUARY 2 TO EPIPHANY
FRIDAY

Signs Without Tracks

WORD

I, the LORD, have called you for the victory of justice,
I have grasped you by the hand;
I formed you, and set you
as a covenant of the people
a light for the nations,

> *To open the eyes of the blind,*
>   *to bring out prisoners from confinement,*
>   *and from the dungeon, those who live in darkness*
>   (Isa 42:6-7).

REFLECTION

In *The Forgiveness of Sin,* which I coauthored with theologian Tad Guzie, I recall this experience from my first pastorate:

> I remember approaching a railroad-crossing sign on a country road. The sign said something to me—slow down! I looked to see if a train were approaching. Seeing none, I passed the sign and was surprised to discover that the tracks had been removed.
>
> I chuckled at the thought that here was a sign which signified nothing, except to recall that trains once ran here. I have been over that road many times since. I no longer "stop, look, and listen," or even slow down. In fact I don't even look at the sign anymore because I know that there is no reason to stop, look, and listen. The sign is useless because the tracks are not there.[31]

Although I wrote this story in order to invite a fuller understanding of sacraments, I repeat it here with reference to a fuller meaning of both Christmas and Epiphany. A preoccupation with Christmas with but a nod to Epiphany makes no more sense than a sign without tracks. Signs must be linked to their reality. Without the reality they signify, signs are little more than exercises in nostalgia.

Christmas without Epiphany is a failure to embody the implications of Christ's birth in our lives. Epiphany calls us to be, so to speak, the "sign" and the "tracks" of Christmas and Epiphany's proclamation of Christ's presence in the world. Christmas proclaims Christ's birth in the past, while Epiphany proclaims Christ's birth *now*! In reality, both are one.

Christmas invites us to ponder the identity of Christ; Epiphany invites us to ponder the wonder that we have been called to share the identity of Christ. When Isaiah proclaimed the coming of the Messiah, he linked him to the people of Israel called to be signs and stewards of justice. Speaking of the Messiah, Isaiah declares:

> Here is my servant whom I uphold,
>   my chosen one with whom I am pleased,

Upon whom I have put my spirit;
>> he shall bring forth justice to the nations,
Not crying out, not shouting,
>> not making his voice heard in the street (Isa 42:1-2).

But this Messiah was not sent to be the sole dispenser of "justice to the nations." Isaiah linked him to God's chosen people:

Thus says God, the LORD,
>> who created the heavens and stretched them out,
>> who spreads out the earth with its crops,
Who gives breath to its people
>> and spirit to those who walk on it:
I, the LORD, have called you for the victory of justice,
>> I have grasped you by the hand;
I formed you, and set you
>> as a covenant of the people,
>> a light for the nations,
To open the eyes of the blind,
>> to bring out prisoners from confinement,
>> and from the dungeon, those who live in darkness
>> (Isa 42:5-7).

In this light, the feast of Epiphany challenges us to embody in our time the servanthood Christ embodied in Bethlehem's manger. We are called to be, with Christ, both the sign and the reality of God's covenant. God sent Jesus into the world for the same reason that all of humankind was created—to be "a light for the nations." We were created a light to expose injustice and, as a light, to reveal God's love and compassion. This is the light with which we must labor to "open the eyes of the blind, to bring out prisoners from confinement, and from the dungeon, those who live in darkness." As we ponder Christ's servant-presence in the manger, Epiphany challenges us to *manifest* Christ's servant-presence in our time. We are challenged to be, in Christ, the way, the truth, and the life for all who live in darkness. Our call to be the light of justice is the reason Christ was born in Bethlehem.

QUESTIONS FOR YOUR REFLECTION

1. While all of us rightfully detest hypocrisy, in what way do we encourage it when we scrupulously attend to signs but leave their

reality untouched? What are some "signs without tracks" situations you have observed?

2. Humor can be defined as the difference between what we think reality is and what it really is. Concerning those who see no humor in the discrepancy between "signs" and no "tracks," what can be said about their understanding of sacraments?

3. "Epiphany" means "manifestation." In what way are the works of justice the manifestation of Christ's ongoing birth in our world and in our time? Who are today's "wise" men and women?

4. When the meaning of Christmas is not associated with the meaning of Epiphany, why will Christmas and consumerism invariably be the spouses of an unhappy marriage?

FROM JANUARY 2 TO EPIPHANY
SATURDAY

The Beauty That Lies Beneath the Ashes

WORD

> *. . . a diadem instead of ashes . . .* (Isa 61:3).

REFLECTION

When I saw a shelf my mother had salvaged from a pile of coal and corncobs, I doubted her wisdom. Though made of oak, the shelf gave evidence of its companionship with coal and cobs. When my equally doubtful father asked, "Bea, what in the world do you see in that piece of junk?" my doubt was confirmed. With a twinkle in her eye, my mother replied, "John, beneath this 'piece of junk' lies a beautiful piece of oak. I am certain that with sandpaper and sweat, you will see what I mean."

Well, after countless evenings of sandpaper and sweat, all of us saw the unfolding of a beauty hidden for many years beneath neglect. I no longer doubted my mother's wisdom, which had pierced the shelf's appearance of junk. Sixty years later this shelf's beauty, evidence of the family's loving care, has confirmed that wisdom wedded to remembrance will reveal a beauty rescued from the identity of junk.

The feast of Epiphany invites us to remember that God's wisdom has seen through the ashes of humankind's companionship with sinfulness to behold a diadem of beauty no eye has seen, no ear has heard (see 1 Cor 2:9). This beauty, infinitely beyond imagination but no less real, is humankind's likeness to God. Beneath the ashes of humankind's sinfulness, Isaiah caught a glimpse of what God's wisdom beholds in the recesses of humanity's likeness to God. From the voice of this great prophet there pours forth an avalanche of wisdom mirroring God's vision of human purpose:

> The spirit of the Lord God is upon me . . .
> To place on those who mourn in Zion
>   a diadem instead of ashes,
> To give them oil of gladness in place of mourning,
>   a glorious mantle instead of a listless spirit.
> They will be called oaks of justice,
>   planted by the LORD to show his glory (Isa 61:1, 3).

Wisdom is a priceless gift of God's Spirit. It enables us to distinguish humanity's "oaks of justice" from the ashes of its "listless spirit." Yes, we are God's "oaks of justice," whose beauty of God-likeness, once buried beneath the ashes of sinfulness, gave humanity the appearance of "junk." Yet Isaiah calls us to understand that we have been "planted by the LORD to show [God's] glory." We are God's epiphany. Our purpose in this life is to be the reality signified by that great mystery of faith. We have been created with the vocation of witnessing to the marvelous exchange of God's divinity for our humanity. St. Augustine exclaims, "God became [human] so that [humanity] might become God."[32]

How does this exchange come to be? The Church insists that the paschal mystery is the center of the mysteries of faith. It is the pilgrimage we make from the "not yet" glory of God's hidden presence to God's "already" glory waiting to be manifested in our lives. Because Christ has been raised, the beauty of God's glory is "already" present; because we have yet to carry the cross of disengagement from the illusions of this world's glory, God's glory remains "yet" to be seen. It groans to be revealed in the epiphany of our creaturehood, called to be the witnesses of its meaning. God bids us to make the pilgrimage by which the seeds of glory sown in our crosses become the reality of glory reaped in the likeness of Christ's resurrection.

Poor self-esteem and its depression are evidence that humankind's destiny to be God's epiphany is either not understood or not accepted. An answer to the yearly question, Why do so many people become depressed after Christmas? might be traced to our tendency to isolate Christmas from Epiphany. When Epiphany's implications for human dignity are ignored by our refusal to make the paschal pilgrimage from Bethlehem to Calvary, the epiphany that raises self-esteem from the self-indulgence of Christmas nostalgia remains a stranger in our midst.

If Christmas is no more than a yearly diversion from our illusion of reality, we ought not be surprised at the depression that ensues. The ultimate meaning of humanity can only be found in the meaning that Christ's incarnation gave to our humanity. It was not his intention to confine the incarnation to Bethlehem's manger. The star over that manger reached out to the nations. Christ longed to be born again in the hearts of the wise who have seen their destiny to be the epiphany of God's light for all the nations. If we fail to believe this "amazing grace," the fruit of that failure may well be one of the reasons for the post-Christmas depression that arises from our reluctance to journey from Christmas to Epiphany.

The feast of Epiphany invites us to reach beyond the confines of Bethlehem. It summons us to make the pilgrimage of the paschal mystery. It asks us to open the eyes of wisdom so that we might discern more fully the beauty of our humanity, created to be the epiphany of God's radiant beauty. Truly we possess the diadem of God's glory. Why, then, should we doubt the wisdom of God, who created us to be the epiphany of that glory?

QUESTIONS FOR YOUR REFLECTION

1. Humility is above all a faithfulness to truth. What gifts, then, do you possess as credentials for being "oaks of justice planted by the LORD to show his glory"?

2. Why is faith in humanity's call to be God's epiphany a strengthening of our faith in the meaning of Christmas? How does failure to recognize the shining star of our talents and charisms prevent us from grasping Christmas' exaltation of human dignity?

3. What purpose of human life qualifies us to be "oaks of justice"? How do we fail that purpose when we settle for a "humility" akin to poor self-esteem?

4. In the course of your lifetime, who have been for you "oaks of justice planted by the LORD to show [God's] glory"? In what way have these people manifested God's presence? What aspects of your personhood's self-esteem have they called forth?

JANUARY 6, OR THE SUNDAY BETWEEN JANUARY 2
AND JANUARY 8
EPIPHANY

Epiphany: Compass for Christmas in the Darkness

WORD

No longer shall the sun
be your light by day.
Nor the brightness of the moon
shine upon you at night;
The LORD shall be your light forever,
your God shall be your glory (Isa 60:19-20).

REFLECTION

One sunny autumn afternoon, a seasoned fisherman and I "put out into deep waters" of a large Minnesota lake. Little did I realize that Isaiah's image of a sunless day was just ahead! With frightening suddenness, a thick fog enveloped us so that "no longer [was] the sun [our] light by day."

My companion's calm composure did not reflect my panic-like feelings as I pondered our plight. Undisturbed, the elderly gentleman lit his pipe as he continued to fish and weave stories about the good old days when the strength of men and the size of fish vied for supremacy. The fright that I endeavored to hide behind a facade of ho-hum chagrin moved me to interrupt the fisherman's tall tales. In a voice that tried to hide my panic I asked, "Mike, fog like this makes it hard to find the way back, don't you think?" My companion exploded with laughter. "Well lad," he said as he pointed to the compass I had not noticed, "if I didn't have that guide in the darkness, I'd be scared too. Come on, let's fish. The compass will get us back home." I relaxed, caught a couple of fish, and listened again to the weaver of tales, whose one and only truth was his word that the compass would "get us back home."

This story of a compass in the darkness suggests the reason why the Church celebrates the mystery of Epiphany. Today she invites us to look beyond Bethlehem's light to the light of the compass that illumines Christ's presence in our world of darkness. The feast of Epiphany calls us to fix our eyes on the Church. Her embodiment of Christ is the compass that paves our way to the likeness of God, in whose image of light we have been called to witness. The Church's claim to be the the body of Christ relates to Epiphany in the same way that Christ's claim to be human relates to the feast of his nativity. It is not fantasy to see the Church as Isaiah's vision for Jerusalem:

> Rise up in splendor, O Jerusalem! Your light has come,
>> the glory of the Lord shines upon you.
> See, darkness covers the earth,
>> and thick clouds cover the peoples;
> But upon you the LORD shines,
>> and over you appears his glory.
> Nations shall walk by your light,
>> and kings by your shining radiance.
> Raise your eyes and look about;
>> they all gather and come to you:
> Your sons come from afar,
>> and your daughters in the arms of their nurses (Isa 60:1-4).

The isolation of Christmas from its moorings to Epiphany may explain why the Church is sometimes isolated from her role to be both light and compass in the world's darkness. Those who look for Bethlehem's light through the eyes of nostalgia give evidence of their refusal to accept the Church's role to be light and compass today. A fellow diocesan priest, speaking in behalf of an elderly "Epiphany Priest," who died near the feast of Epiphany, addresses the Church's mission to be the manifestation of Christ's birth:

> We have just celebrated the great feast of Epiphany. It always amazes me [that] the churches are totally packed for Christmas Masses, [but] for Epiphany, it's back to normal. . . . I look for an answer to this dilemma.
>
> One aspect of the answer might be that Christmas allows us to look back [while] Epiphany demands that we look forward. Christmas allows us to go to Bethlehem, gaze at an innocent baby with his virginal parents, hear the angels sing, and experience the simple joy of shepherds—it's warm, it's beautiful, it touches us for a moment, and then we can go on with our lives. . . .
>
> Epiphany, on the other hand, calls us to follow the star, to make a [pilgrimage], and more profoundly, to "be the star" that leads others to the Messiah and King. It challenges our faith and it calls us to make response to the truth of Bethlehem."[33]

Christmas and Epiphany are one. To confine Christmas to its historical setting without Epiphany's challenge to be witnesses of Christ's presence diminishes the splendor of human dignity. Christmas longs for our ecclesial consent to "be the star" that with the compass of our faith and obedience, guides God's people on their pilgrimage "back home" through this world's darkness.

Christmas asks for more than polite assent to incarnation's doctrinal truth. In a world of darkness our security lies not in the mere availability of a compass. Our security lies in the freedom to *be* the compass that guides humankind from darkness to the light of Christ. When we accept the ecclesial responsibility of uniting Christmas and Epiphany, our ecclesial presence in a world of darkness will be the certainty all nations can count on.

QUESTIONS FOR YOUR REFLECTION

1. How is effectiveness of Christmas' spirituality endangered when the nativity of Christ is celebrated with minimal reference to

Epiphany? Why does the isolation of Christmas from Epiphany make vague our ecclesial role in Christ's ongoing nativity?

2. The light of Christ is present in the Church. How is the Church's effectiveness assured when the members of the Church unite the meaning of nativity to Epiphany?

3. When we give our consent to be the manifestation of Christ's birth, what is required of our dignity to be members of Christ's body?

4. Christmas will have its transforming effect if we link its meaning to Epiphany's meaning. In the light of that assertion, why does the feast of Epiphany enjoy a higher rank than Christmas?

AFTER EPIPHANY TO THE BAPTISM OF THE LORD
MONDAY

"Let's Go for a Walk"

WORD

The Spirit of the Lord has . . . sent me to bring glad tidings to the poor (Luke 4:18).

REFLECTION

I was disappointed the first time I entered St. Peter's Basilica in Rome. It was smaller than I had expected. When I voiced my chagrin, a companion whispered, "Let's go for a walk." Well, we went for a walk; we walked, and walked, and walked. By the time we reached the altar area, a manifestation of St. Peter's immensity had already unfolded within the parameters of my once-paltry perspective.

When the companion pointed out that the distance from the top of the basilica's dome to its floor was approximately a hundred feet longer than a football field, my imagination was staggered. Moreover, he pointed out that lengthwise the basilica's immensity was even more astonishing. For example, New York's St. Patrick's Cathedral, towers and all, could have easily been erected within the altar-apse area of the basilica. He also pointed out that St. Paul's Cathedral in London, with its three-hundred-sixty-five-foot dome, could stand within the interior of St. Peter's Basilica.

The walk I had been invited to take transformed my disappointment into awe.

The experience of St. Peter's manifestation of immensity related to my pondering about Epiphany's meaning. That marvelous mystery, I reflected, is likewise the manifestation of a divine immensity that cannot be contained within the smallness of human perspective. Undoubtedly, the genius of that basilica's architecture is its perspective of smallness, through which we can initially relate to its immensity. Similarly, the genius of Epiphany is its artistry of manifesting God's immensity well within the boundaries of our graced perspective to behold it. Epiphany is eager to remind us that when Christ came to walk with us in our humanity, God's immensity began to unfold in our awe-filled presence.

Epiphany wants to walk with us beyond Christ's historical presence in Bethlehem. Epiphany invites creation to manifest, reveal, and radiate God's glory *now*! It summons all nations to behold the lowliness of Joseph and Mary, to look at a star, to notice its gifts of gold, frankincense, and myrrh, to stand with Christ at Jordan's baptismal waters, and to accompany Christ to Cana, where he transformed the lowliness of water into the fragrance of good wine.

Epiphany's meaning is clear, emphatic, and consistent. She wants no misunderstanding about creation's role as the manifestation of Christ's presence. Her sacraments proclaim that God's real presence is contained in the sacramentality of creation's lowliness so that our faith might grasp God's immensity. St. Peter Chrysologus writes: "In choosing to be born for us, God chose to be known by us. He therefore reveals himself in this way, in order that this great sacrament of his love [Christ's incarnation] may not be an occasion for us of great misunderstanding."[34]

But if the lesser creatures of the universe are called to be the sacramentals of God's immensity, do not the greater creatures of God's image and likeness manifest more nobly the dignity of that calling? This question occupied Jesus' fullest attention as he pondered the meaning of human existence. As Jesus grew in wisdom, age, and grace, so also his human consciousness expanded, making him aware that he was the manifestation of the Father's love to humankind—indeed, he was the incarnate sign of God's love among us. Long before Jesus asked his disciples, "Who do you say I am?" (Matt 16:15), might not he have already pondered, "Who does God say I am?"

Through the prism of God's creation, Jesus came to understand his identity as God's epiphany. He discerned that he was Isaiah's "anointed," sent to proclaim liberty, healing, and the good news of human existence to all whose existence had been crushed by the heel of injustice (see Isa 61:1). Standing before Nazareth's synagogue assembly, he said quite simply:

> The Spirit of the Lord is upon me;
> therefore, he has anointed me.
> He has sent me to bring glad tidings to the poor,
> to proclaim liberty to captives,
> Recovery of sight to the blind
> and release to prisoners,
> To announce a year of favor from the Lord (Luke 4:18-19).

Christ's joy to be the epiphany in our humanity is also our joy to be the epiphany in Christ's divinity. Epiphany's feast pleads with us never to let our sense of lowliness deter us from the awesome mission of sharing Christ's "anointed" mission to be the epiphany of God's immensity. Ought not this very sense of lowliness enliven our faith to say with Christ, "Today this Scripture passage is fulfilled in [our] hearing" (Luke 4:21)? In faith we have only to walk with Jesus in our humanity to proclaim its exalted dignity of being the epiphany of God's immensity.

With Christ, then, "let's go for a walk."

QUESTIONS FOR YOUR REFLECTION

1. What are the implications of Epiphany? Why might these implications be the reason for keeping Christ in Bethlehem?

2. How is Jesus' call to "follow me" an invitation to "go for a walk" with the humanity of Jesus, so that through him, with him, and in him, we might become the manifestation of God's immensity?

3. "Small Is Beautiful" is the title of a book. How do these words apply to us and to Epiphany?

Was It a Mistake?

WORD

No more shall [people] call you "Forsaken,"
or your land "Desolate,"
But you shall be called "My Delight,"
and your land "Espoused."
For the LORD delights in you,
and makes your land his spouse (Isa 62:4).

REFLECTION

The esteem God holds for us is often puzzling. Again and again we experience forsakenness and desolation, when actually we are God's "Delight" and God's "Espoused." And yet, when asked to shoulder responsibilities that ill fit our perception of self-esteem, we feel compelled to ask, "Was it a mistake to ask this of me?"

This was the question uppermost in the mind of Albino Cardinal Luciani, who chose the name John Paul I after he hesitantly but obediently accepted election to his brief papacy in 1978. Commenting on the newly elected Pope's doubts about his suitability, John Cornwell writes: "There is ample evidence that John Paul believed from the outset that his election had been a mistake and that his Papacy was doomed. He longed to die, he prayed and begged God to die, and he was convinced that it would not be long before his wish was granted. . . . Without seeking [the papacy], lobbying for it or even vaguely suspecting it, Luciani at age sixty-five was placed in one of the world's most demanding executive hot seats."[35]

There is no doubt that newly elected Pope John Paul I was appalled at the disparity between his felt inability to shoulder papal responsibilities and the sublime esteem with which he viewed the papacy. It is obvious that he stood before God as one "Forsaken" and "Desolate" and saw his election as a mistake. Was it a mistake?

If his doubts did no more than raise our own consciousness about obedience to the faith of shouldering the responsibilities of the Church's identity, his election for the brief papacy of thirty-three days was not a mistake.

If the Church's human identity is seen as the sole foundation for the discipleship of God's own Son, then doubt about shouldering responsibilities for a solely human Church is in order. But if the Church calls us to include her vertical dimension of divine presence as integral to *our* identity, can any of us dismiss baptism's foundation of ecclesial membership as a "mistake"? Must our faith-less perceptions of human inability to shoulder the responsibilities of a divinely endowed Church be the sole determinant for obedience to God's Word? It is not, and neither was Cardinal Luciani's election to the papacy a mistake!

The Church's horizontal identity is espoused to God's Word. The espousal that constitutes the Church's identity challenges our perceptions of self-esteem. Decisions to do God's will measured only by our measurement of self-esteem or its lack is the mistake of mistakes. Why? Because such decisions are based on egocenteredness. When we respond to God's will only in this light, we prevent birth to unfolding manifestations of divine presence that *God sees* in the lowly mangers of our humanity. Faith is the capacity for us to see that hiddenness and act on it.

God seeks the very lowliness that this world measures worthless. Obedience is at its pinnacle when we seek for what no eye can see or no ear can hear. Those who are graced to obey God's Word are graced to embrace the "Forsaken" and "Desolate" as the "Delight" and the "Espoused" of God's esteem. The Church never hesitates to renew Isaiah's joyful cry:

> No more shall [people] call you "Forsaken,"
>   or your land "Desolate,"
> But you shall be called "My Delight,"
>   and your land "Espoused."
> For the LORD delights in you,
>   and makes your land his spouse.

It may be more than coincidence that at the midpoint between Christmas and Epiphany the Church joyously exclaims: "O marvelous exchange! [Our] Creator has become [human], born of a virgin. We have been made sharers in the divinity of Christ who humbled himself to share in our humanity."[36]

This antiphon's astonishing assertion that in Mary's motherhood both God and humanity have *exchanged* identities overwhelms us. Without faith's vertical place in the Church, her membership would doubtless respond, This is a mistake! But with obedient faith, the call to make this exchange is *not* a mistake! Jesus made this exchange so that in our obedience to his "marvelous exchange," we might be reowned to share God's identity. Nor is God's longing for our lowliness a mistake. God begs for our deserts of forsakenness and desolation so that we might become the gardens of "Delight" in his kingdom's "land."

"O marvelous exchange!" This glad cry of the Church invites us to see with the eyes of faith the glory of our lowliness. When we measure the glory of human purpose only by this world's credentials for glory, we block the way Jesus chose as the Epiphany of God's glory in the world. In our lowliness, we have been made the epiphany of divine glory. This is the dignity God gladly bestows in exchange for the lowliness of our humanity.

The epiphany of God's presence in John Paul I's brief papacy left an indelible mark on the lives of millions. His election was evidence that God's call for his lowliness to be the "Servant of Servants" was no mistake. Nor is our call to be God's epiphany a mistake. God calls for our consent to be the "Bethlehem" of Christ's incarnation in exchange for God's unfolding epiphany in the world *today!*

QUESTIONS FOR YOUR REFLECTION

1. How are God's gifts of faith and hope made ineffective when our perception of "mistake" becomes the final word of our response to God? What is meant by the proverb "God writes straight with crooked lines"?

2. In what way did Pope John Paul I's obedience manifest the rightness of God's way within the "crooked lines" of that newly elected Pope's perception of his fitness for the papacy?

3. Why are both the horizontal and vertical dimensions of the Church's identity absolutely essential for our role of being epiphany to the world? How is epiphany endangered when only one

or the other of these two dimensions is seen as the Church's total identity?

AFTER EPIPHANY TO THE BAPTISM OF THE LORD
WEDNESDAY

A Sparrow in the Hand . . .

WORD

On the feast of the Savior's birth, the earth rejoiced because it bore the Lord in a manger; but on today's feast of the Epiphany it is the sea that is glad and leaps for joy; the sea is glad because it receives the blessing of holiness in the river Jordan (St. Proclus of Constantinople, bishop).[37]

REFLECTION

One of my mother's proverbs helped me appreciate what I possessed rather than what I lacked. She never tired of saying, "A sparrow in the hand is worth more than two in the bush." During the dark days of the Great Depression this proverb proved to be providential. Its light during those depressing years opened my eyes to a deeper meaning of blessing of which I was formerly unaware. In due time, her frequent recitation of "A sparrow in the hand . . ." prepared me for a deeper meaning of epiphany as the blessedness of humanity.

Epiphany's meaning of God's manifestation unfolds when we seriously explore human purpose and the dignity that is its fruit. Epiphany proclaims the good news that God's presence longs to be manifested and magnified not only in our humanity but also in all of God's creation. When the Church blesses persons, places, and things, she does not bestow a manifestation of God's presence that creation does not possess. The Church blesses in order to *acknowledge* the manifestation of God's presence mirrored in creation. Creation's manifestation of Christ is the credential for dignity that Epiphany proclaims.

A sermon by St. Proclus reveals the thoughts of a man whose spirituality obviously rested on this cornerstone of Epiphany's proclamation: "Christ appeared in the world, and bringing beauty out of disarray, gave it luster and joy. He bore the world's sin and crushed the world's enemy. He sanctified the fountains of waters and enlightened the minds of [all]. Into the fabric of miracles he interwove ever greater miracles."[38]

"Into the fabric of miracles. . . ." For St. Proclus, miracles are not feats of a divine magic that "sanctified the fountains of waters." Rather, he regards miracles as revelations of God's presence in creation celebrated by the birth of Christ. St. Paul writes, "I consider the sufferings of the present to be as nothing compared with the glory to be revealed in us. . . . The whole created world eagerly awaits the revelation of the [children] of God. . . . Creation groans and is in agony even until now" (Rom 8:18-19, 22).

The marvels of Christ's presence wait only for our consent to accept the birth pangs of his hidden presence, groaning for manifestation through us, with us, and in us. These are the sufferings, St. Paul insists, that announce the glad tidings of Christ's manifestation, which the Church's blessings of all things are eager to acknowledge.

This writer never tires of calling his readers' attention to the stunning beauty of Gerard Manley Hopkins' poem "God's Grandeur."

> The world is charged with the grandeur of God.
> It will flame out, like shining from shook foil;
>
> . . .
>
> nature is never spent;
> There lives the dearest freshness deep down things.[39]

It is this "dearest freshness [of] deep down things" that the blessings of the Church call us to acknowledge with faith's eyes so that Epiphany's ritual might challenge us to become Epiphany's reality. St. Proclus perceives the meaning of Epiphany's blessing in all of creation: "On the feast of the Savior's birth, the earth rejoiced because it bore the Lord in a manger; but on today's feast of the Epiphany it is the sea that is glad and leaps for joy; the sea is glad because it receives the blessing of holiness in the river of Jordan."[40]

Epiphany invites us to look through the eyes of sacramentality. This unique mark of Catholic identity gathers the whole world to cherish the blessedness of persons, places, and things. Sacramentality is the Church's insistence that Christ's manifestation is not locked into ritual recollections of Epiphany's historical event. Sacramentality calls for our consent to *be* the good news that all of creation ever groans to reveal.

The Catholic Church welcomes opportunities to bless *everything* save sin. Why? Because she is eager to acknowledge the sacredness—the sacramentality—of everything. It is through our awareness of creation's sacredness that the beauty of Christ's presence will be revealed in *this* world, as well as in the next. The feast of the Epiphany is the good news that God's manifestation of marvels is not outside our reach. "No," exclaimed the author of Deuteronomy, "it is something very near to you, already in your mouths and in your hearts; you have only to carry it out" (Deut 30:14).

QUESTIONS FOR YOUR REFLECTION

1. When I asked a young man if the Church's blessing of his new car guaranteed a safety it didn't possess, he indicated that this was his understanding. In the light of the above reflection, how would you respond to the young man?

2. In our world so endangered by pollution, why is a renewed effort to explore ever-deeper meanings of sacramentality vitally necessary for people of faith in roles of environmental leadership?

3. Asked by an emperor to bless his decision to wage war, a pope replied that he blessed peace, not war. How was the pope's response consistent with the Church's meaning of sacramentality?

4. How would a renewed perspective of Epiphany as the manifestation of God's presence in creation allow us to expect miracles we once regarded as outside our domain?

"The Holy Ghost over the Bent World"

WORD

Your holy cities have become a desert,
  Zion is a desert, Jerusalem a waste.
Our holy and glorious temple
  in which our fathers praised you
Has been burned with fire;
  all that was dear to us is laid waste (Isa 64:9-10).

REFLECTION

"Acres of Diamonds" is the tale of a man who sold his farm so that he might search elsewhere for diamonds. The search was a failure and he became a penniless vagrant. Torn between his wounded ego's craving for nostalgia and the yearning to be freed from the depths of depression, he returned to the farm that had once been his pride and joy. As he walked the acres of his youth, his nostalgia was assaulted by a despair that saw nothing to live for. Tragically, he took his life.

Later in the day the farmer discovered the man's body and, finding no evidences of identification, proceeded to bury him. With the grave almost finished, the farmer's spade struck a large diamond. This was the first of many found later in the acres of diamonds that its former possessor had exchanged for a grave.

In "Acres of Diamonds" we see the waste of exchanging one's hidden riches for fantasies that betray the riches of undisclosed identity. Both humor and tragedy are in this story. The tragedy is apparent. Not apparent but quite real is the humor of a facade that masks the marbles we're bound to lose for the diamonds we already possess.

"All . . . is laid waste," the Church exclaims as we near the end of Christmas and Epiphany's season of joy. Is this a gloom that suggests the irony of both tragedy and humor at the climax of this season of joy? Of course it is. As this season ends, the Church repeats Isaiah's dire warning about creation's danger of being "laid waste" by those who forget the joy of their dignity as companions of God's Holy Spirit. Indeed, Isaiah cries out, "The Spirit of God is upon me" (Isa 61:1). How tragic, the prophet seems to say, to lay waste creation in pursuit of a fantasy that betrays in exchange for the Spirit's presence in our "acres of diamonds" existence. At the same time, humor awaits those who have the humility to recognize fantasy's facade as a colossal "sting." For those who admit, "I've been had," conversion is inevitable!

The Church praises creation's manifestation of God's presence as she remembers that it is God's Spirit who unveils that presence. Creation, *of itself,* has no power to be the epiphany. Only when men and women of faith acknowledge the indwelling presence of God's Spirit in all of creation can they recognize that they possess the riches of God's presence. What a waste to search for these riches in fantasy's land!

Jesus clothed himself with humanity so that humanity might be clothed with the Spirit of God. This is the Spirit who overshadowed Mary at Nazareth and Jesus at the Jordan River. In the Spirit's presence the Father embraced Mary as she said, "Let it be done to me as you say" (Luke 1:38). The Father embraced Jesus when he said, "This is my beloved Son. My favor rests on him" (Matt 3:17). In this twofold embrace, God embraced all of humanity.

Today the Church asks us to remember Isaiah's vision of a creation "laid waste," so that we might never forget that searching for fantasy's facades will be fruitless in their "desert" of futility. How futile to search for riches *beneath* human dignity in exchange for God's riches *consistent* with human dignity! St. Cyril of Alexandria remarks: "In a plan of surpassing beauty the Creator of the universe decreed the renewal of all things in Christ. In his design for restoring human nature to its original condition, he gave a promise that he would pour out on it the Holy Spirit along with his other gifts, for otherwise, our nature could not enter once more into the peaceful possession of those gifts."[41]

When imperishability is exchanged for perishability's unquenchable thirsts, the earth is laid waste. Gerard Manley Hopkins is aware of Isaiah's dire warnings about humankind's misuse of this world's goodness. He asks:

> Why do men then now not reck his rod?
> Generations have trod, have trod, have trod;
>   And all is seared with trade; bleared, smeared with toil;
>   And wears man's smudge and shares man's smell: the soil
> Is bare now, nor can foot feel, being shod.[42]

Had Hopkins ended with this seemingly near-despair perspective of an earth laid waste, "God's Grandeur" might have passed as trivial pursuit. Happily, Hopkins ends his poem on a note of joyful hope. Beyond his perception of a world "seared with trade" and "smeared with toil," Hopkins transcends the consequences of self-indulgence:

> And though the last lights off the black West went
>   Oh, morning, at the brown brink eastward, springs—
> Because the Holy Ghost over the bent
> World broods with warm breast and with ah! bright wings."[43]

"The Holy Ghost over the bent world broods." God's Spirit "broods with warm breast" over vistas of unexplored "freshness deep down things," waiting to be discovered as the manifestation of God's presence. Hopkins may also envision the Spirit's "bright wings" hovering over Christ as he rescued our humanity from its Spirit-less existence. This is the Spirit who has never ceased hovering over the "freshness deep down things" hidden within our creaturehood. This hovering Spirit invites all of us to be the epiphany of our Father, who says of us, "This is my beloved [people]. My favor rests on [them]" (Matt 3:17).

QUESTIONS FOR YOUR REFLECTION

1. Conversion is a return to what we were created to possess. How is the parable of the prodigal son like the story "Acres of Diamonds"? Where does the similarity end?

2. The concerns of those who choose to respect creation challenge us to a consistent ethic of life. How is this ethic of life consistent with creation's destiny to be God's epiphany?

3. The heresy of Jansenism was condemned because it degraded the Church's humanity. How would the Church's failure to condemn that heresy have rendered ineffective the Church's epiphany message? Conversely, how would the exclusion of the Church's divine dimension have endangered creation's destiny to be an instrument of epiphany?

4. In what way is the Holy Spirit's overshadowing presence over Mary's humanity an important link to our understanding of the Spirit's hovering presence over Jesus in the Jordan River?

AFTER EPIPHANY TO THE BAPTISM OF THE LORD
FRIDAY

An Answer Correct but Incomplete

WORD

> *Lo, I am about to create new heavens*
> *and a new earth. . . .*
> *For I create Jerusalem to be a joy*
> *and its people to be a delight* (Isa 65:17, 18).

REFLECTION

According to the Baltimore Catechism, we were created to know, love, serve, and be happy with God for all eternity. This is a correct answer. But I wonder if it is complete. The catechism suggests a perspective of human purpose that appears to rule out the Creator's perspective.

What if we looked at the catechism's answer from God's point of view? Isn't it also true that *God* longs to know us, love us, serve us, and be happy with us for all eternity? Far from ruling out what we learned, that response offers us the beautiful image of a nuptial relationship between the Creator and the created.

The nuptial image enables us to see that *we are lovable*. In the light of the Creator's longing for us to be the epiphany of divine love, *we* experience the longing to know, love, serve, and share God's companionship for all eternity. We understand more fully Christ's gentle words: "Come to me, all you who are weary and find life burdensome, and I will refresh you. Take my yoke upon your shoulders and learn from me, for I am gentle and humble of heart. Your souls will find rest, for my yoke is easy and my burden light" (Matt 11:28-30).

How unburdening the joy of being recognized as lovable and essential to God's passionate love for us! The old song "You're Nobody 'til Somebody Loves You" has survived not because its melody is classic but because its words are. To know, love, and serve God becomes the vocation of vocations, because God's purpose of human life calls us to be the epiphany that radiates from a healthy self-esteem. That vocation grows from the realization that God has created us in order to reveal through us, with us, and in us the divine identity. We are called to be epiphany not by way of burden but by way of accepting God's never-ending outpouring of love. The pinnacle of faith is our embrace of the simple truth that God loves us because "God *is* love" (1 John 4:8, italics added).

This truth initially escaped the comprehension of John the Baptizer when Jesus presented himself for baptism at the Jordan River. Deeply puzzled because Jesus asked to be baptized, John responded, "I should be baptized by you, yet you come to me!" (John 13:14). A saintly bishop comments insightfully on the perplexity of John the Baptizer: "Someone might ask, 'Why would a holy man desire baptism?' Listen to the answer: Christ is baptized, not to be made holy by the water, but to make the water holy, and by his cleansing to purify the water which he touched. For the consecration of Christ involves a more significant consecration of water" (St. Maximus of Turin, bishop).[44]

The baptism of Jesus in Jordan's waters awakens us to *God's* perspective of creation. God sent Jesus so that his presence might awaken all of humanity to creaturehood's role to be the epiphany of God's love. Jesus walked into the water of the Jordan River to cleanse it of the futility to which it was condemned at the beginning of time. Consecrated by Christ's presence to manifest God's esteem for all of creation, the Jordan's waters become Isaiah's joyful news of creation's epiphany role:

> Lo, I am about to create new heavens
>> and a new earth;
> The things of the past shall not be remembered
>> or come to mind.
> Instead, there shall always be rejoicing and happiness
>> in what I create;
> For I create Jerusalem to be a joy
>> and its people to be a delight (Isa 65:17-18).

Isaiah's vision is fulfilled in John the Evangelist: "I saw new heavens and a new earth. . . . I heard a loud voice from the throne cry out: 'This is God's dwelling among [all].' [God] shall dwell with them. . . . [The Lord] shall wipe every tear from their eyes, and there shall be no more death or mourning, crying out or pain, for the former world has passed away" (Rev 21:1, 3, 4).

All the waters of the world are instruments of God's epiphany because God respects and esteems the wholeness of creation. When Christ asked for baptism in the waters of the Jordan, he responded to creation's groaning for the "revelation of the [children] of God" (Rom 8:19). The dignity Jesus conferred upon the waters of the Jordan became the dignity that he bestowed upon all creatures. It is true, Christ did not need to be baptized! But creation did need to be freed from the serpent's lie of creation's alleged right to sovereignty. In choosing to be baptized in the Jordan's waters, Jesus unveiled the manifestation of God's favor to humanity.

No, the Baltimore Catechism's perspective is not incorrect. But wedded to the Creator's point of view, it becomes complete.

QUESTIONS FOR YOUR REFLECTION

1. How does the image of a nuptial relationship between God and humankind motivate us to know, love, and serve God on earth so that we might share God's companionship forever?

2. Why is our role to manifest the identity of God a sign that *all* of us are lovable? How does our role to be the epiphany enhance self-esteem? How does it challenge the exercise of faith?

3. How would you explain why Jesus asked John the Baptizer for baptism in the Jordan River?

"Are You Really Serious, Father?"

WORD

I come to gather nations of every language; they shall come and see my glory. I will set a sign among them; from them I will send fugitives to the nations . . . to the distant coastlands that have never heard of my fame, or seen my glory; and they shall proclaim my glory among the nations. They shall bring all your brethren from all the nations as an offering to the LORD . . . (Isa 66:18-20).

REFLECTION

Before sitting down to dinner at a parish celebration, I introduced myself to those seated nearby. A man directly across from me looked puzzled as I extended my hand.

"Are you really serious, Father?" he asked with chiding eyes.

It was my turn to be puzzled as I asked, "What makes you think I'm not serious?"

"Because," he continued, "I'm Joe What's-His-Name and we were classmates for four years at some high school whose name I don't recall."

His hilarious touché ended my puzzlement about his identity, and we broke up in laughter. I failed to recognize a classmate because from graduation day until this awkward moment forty years later, he and I had been out of touch.

Our reunion awakened me to a basis for religion's integrity. Relationships are religion's essence, and changes in religion must be expected. Relationships do not stand still! Why? Because the life that reveals them never ceases reaching out for a relationship with God, life's only author. True life is recognized only by those who keep in touch with God. For religion to be authentic, people must gather again and again.

That gathering is the Church. Jesus Christ commissioned the Church to "go into the whole world and proclaim the good news to all creation" (Mark 16:15). When that infant assembly had received the Holy Spirit, they recognized that Jesus was the Word of "good news," calling all men and women to gather to be the likeness of God's Trinitarian identity. The Church had been commissioned to be the assembly of Christ's presence so that his final prayer might be fulfilled: "I have given them the glory you gave me that they may be one, as we are one . . . so [that the world will know] that you sent me" (John 17:22, 23). How accurately Jesus renewed God's message to Isaiah: "I come to gather nations of every language; they shall come and see my glory. I will set a sign among them; from them I will send fugitives to the nations . . . and they shall proclaim my glory among the nations. They shall bring all your brethren from all the nations as an offering to the LORD."

When Jesus commissioned his disciples, he clearly stated his desire for the Church to be the epiphany of God's communion of three persons. God *is* a community of divine persons. Christ founded the Church so that here upon earth, all men and women might gather to celebrate the joy of God's communion and their epiphany of that communion here upon earth.

Why is frequency of ecclesial gathering necessary? Because our assembly with Christ transforms us to be the way, the truth, and the life of God's identity. Through our gathering with Christ, we grow, change, develop, and are transformed to become the triune likeness of Father, Son, and Holy Spirit. We are on a pilgrimage, and we gather to be nourished by Christ and to be rested in Christ.

The Church draws our attention to another perspective of epiphany, the wedding feast at Cana. For this perspective to be fruitful, she asks us not to dwell on the details of water becoming wine. She asks us to remember that Christ visited the Cana wedding for the same reason that he visited this world. He came to be the epiphany of humankind's intimacy with God and to manifest God's longing for intimacy with his assembled people. Christ came to Cana's wedding to celebrate the commitment of two people vowing their nuptial intimacy as the epiphany of God.

At Cana, Jesus did not transform water into wine to be dramatic. He signified through this marvelous exchange love's transforming power in matrimony's exchange. Jesus revealed his longing to be with diversity so that unity might be unveiled. "O marvelous exchange! . . . We have been made sharers in the divinity of Christ who humbled himself to share our humanity."[45]

Epiphany calls us to gather frequently with Christ so that we might recognize, through the eyes of faith, the relationship of human purpose to the Church's mission of gathering the members of his body. With the water of baptism we are graced to be transformed into the likeness of Christ's saving blood. With bread and wine we joyfully celebrate the good news that this transformation is a reality. Daily the Church exclaims:

> From age to age you gather a people to yourself, so that from east to west a perfect offering may be made to the glory of your name (Eucharistic Prayer III).[46]

And again:

> We thank you for counting us worthy to stand in your presence and serve you. May all of us who share the body and blood of Christ be brought together in unity by the Holy Spirit (Eucharistic Prayer II).[47]

We are obliged to gather at the Eucharist so that we might recognize a new identity taking place in our assembly. This new identity is Christ's intimacy with God and God's with us. It is the identity of a people whose transformation into the likeness of Christ is likened not only to water changed into wine but also wine changed into the Blood of Christ. For those who faithfully assemble in the name of Christ, there will always be faith's recognition that "the choice wine" of Christ's identity has been kept "until now."

QUESTIONS FOR YOUR REFLECTION

1. St. Luke records that after Christ's resurrection, two of his disciples did not recognize him until "they had come to know him in the breaking of the bread" (Luke 24:35). What does this post-resurrection story say about our commitment to be the Church's Eucharistic assembly? How is our gathering to worship an epiphany?

2. Why is Church a necessity for life here upon earth? Why will Church not be a necessity in heaven?

74

3. What is the connection between Church and religion? If "Church" means "assembly," how is the failure to assemble at the Eucharist a detriment to religion?

4. The image of God is oneness of three divine persons. How would a deeper awareness of the Church as the likeness of God's communitarian image motivate all of us to take seriously the obligation to gather for worship?

THE SUNDAY AFTER EPIPHANY
BAPTISM OF THE LORD

Epiphany: God's Love in Search of a Word

WORD

I, the LORD, have called you for the victory of justice" (Isa 42:6).

REFLECTION

On my desk is a notepad whose pages offer this thought-filled expression: "Music is love in search of a word." I like this assertion not only for what it says about music but also for what it suggests about epiphany. Epiphany is likewise God's love in search of a Word.

In Bethlehem, God's love found the Word lying in a manger. But the Word, wrapped in humanity, was subject to its limitations. The humanity of God's Word, lying in a manger and suject to time and space, reached out to all of creation to be the Word of God's love manifested until the end of time.

Epiphany's love in search of a Word began by reaching out to a star above the manger, to the waters of the Jordan, and to the water made wine at the wedding feast of Cana. Its search began with creation because creation had never ceased groaning for the revelation of the children of God (see Rom 8:19, 22). These groans turned to joy when the peoples of all nations discovered that *they*, in union with Christ, enjoyed the dignity of being the epiphany of God's identity in search of their Word. Yes, we are the light of the star, the cleansing of the Jordan, and the joy of a humanity transformed by love!

Love's search for a Word has never ceased because God's immensity is infinitely more than humanity can embrace. The mission of God's love in search of a Word has reached out unceasingly. From the depths of injustice in the garden of Eden, love has never ceased searching for the justice that humanity was created to reveal. Of its servant, Isaiah speaks:

> Here is my servant whom I uphold,
>> my chosen one with whom I am pleased,
> Upon whom I have put my spirit;
>> he shall bring forth justice to the nations,
> Not crying out, not shouting,
>> not making his voice heard in the street.
> A bruised reed he shall not break,
>> and a smouldering wick he shall not quench,
> Until he establishes justice on the earth;
>> the coastlands will wait for his teaching (Isa 42:1-4).

It must not go unnoticed that Isaiah's servant of justice also embraced a people called to be the manifestation of God's covenant for all who live in darkness:

> I, the LORD, have called you for the victory of justice,
>> I have grasped you by the hand;
> I formed you, and set you
>> as a covenant of the people,
>> a light for the nations,
> To open the eyes of the blind,
>> to bring out prisoners from confinement,
>> and from the dungeon, those who live in darkness (Isa 42:6-7).

Is it arrogant to claim that we are the light of Christ? Not if we respond to faith's good news that Christ, the light of the world, has chosen our humanity as the medium of his light to the nations. St.

Gregory Nazianzus asserted this beautiful truth when he says, "Christ is bathed in light; let us also be bathed in light."[48]

Is it arrogant to say that we are the waters of refreshment for those who thirst for justice? Not if we believe that our humanity is graced to be the refreshing presence of Jesus in this world. Surely a connection between Christ's entry into the water of the Jordan and our entry into the waters of baptism is not small talk.

And finally, is it arrogant to say that we are the "good wine" transformed into the likeness of Christ from the waters of baptism? Not if we believe that we have been called to be the reality of Christ's transforming presence signified by the Eucharist.

The very meaning of humility lies in its capacity to help us understand our vocation to pass over from darkness to light, from death to life, from exile to communion. As the servants of Christ, then, we are called to be the epiphany of God's light, God's life, and God's presence here and now!

Yes, epiphany is love in search of a Word. In Christ, that Word has been found. In us, love's search goes on. We are, indeed, servants of epiphany's search for a Word. God calls us to fill up that which the Word left for our flesh to complete. How insignificant the giftedness of star, water, and wine when compared to humanity's dignity of being the Word for which epiphany never ceases to search. May we never tire of proclaiming, "O marvelous exchange!" That marvel is worth the search!

QUESTIONS FOR YOUR REFLECTION

1. Why did epiphany's search for a Word not stop with the Word lying in a manger?

2. In what way are we the words for which epiphany is searching? How does a poor self-esteem thwart epiphany's search for a Word?

3. At Jesus' baptism in the Jordan, the Holy Spirit hovered over him. At Pentecost, the Spirit descended on the infant Church. Linking these two mysteries of faith, how is Pentecost like Epiphany in terms of love's search for a Word?

4. How do we manifest the virtue of humility when we sincerely believe that we are the epiphany longing to act according to that conviction?

Notes

1. "Sermon on the Nativity of the Lord," *Patrologia Latina. Liturgy of the Hours,* 1:405.

2. Timothy Fitzgerald, "The Time of Christmas Masses," *Liturgy 80* 18 (November–December 1987) 4.

3. "Sermon on the Nativity of the Lord," *Patrologia Latina. Liturgy of the Hours,* 1:405.

4. "Sermon," *Corpus Christianorum Series Latina. Liturgy of the Hours,* 1:1256.

5. "Sermon on the Nativity of the Lord," *Patrologia Latina. Liturgy of the Hours,* 1:404.

6. "The Tractates on the First Letter of St. John," *Patrologia Latina. Liturgy of the Hours,* 1:1266.

7. "Sermon," *Patrologia Latina. Liturgy of the Hours,* 1:1274.

8. *The Oxford Dictionary of Quotations,* 3rd ed. (New York: Oxford University Press, 1979) 517.

9. "Sermon," *Patrologia Latina. Liturgy of the Hours,* 1:1274.

10. Ibid., 1274–1275.

11. Ibid., 1275.

12. Ibid.

13. "Sermon on the Epiphany of the Lord," *Patrologia Latina. Liturgy of the Hours,* 1:446–447.

14. Ibid., 1:447.

15. "On the Refutation of All Heresies," *Patrologia Graeca. Liturgy of the Hours,* 1:460.

16. John J. McIlhon, "This Too Will Pass," *Markings* (Chicago: Thomas More, September 10, 1989).

17. "On the Refutation of All Heresies," *Patrologia Graeca. Liturgy of the Hours,* 1:459.

18. "Sermon on the Nativity of the Lord," *Patrologia Latina. Liturgy of the Hours,* 1:471.

19. Ibid., 1:472.

20. *Mary at the Foot of the Cross* (San Francisco: Ignatius, 1988) 42.

21. *Liturgy of the Hours*, 1:491.

22. "A Letter to Epictetus," *Patrologia Graeca. Liturgy of the Hours*, 1:484.

23. *Mary at the Foot of the Cross*, 43.

24. "On the Holy Spirit," *Patrologia Graeca. Liturgy of the Hours*, 1:504.

25. Ibid.

26. "Treatise on John," *Corpus Christianorum Series Latina. Liturgy of the Hours*, 1:512.

27. Ibid.

28. "Five Hundred Chapters," *Patrologia Graeca. Liturgy of the Hours*, 1:519–520.

29. "From a Sermon," *Patrologia Latina. Liturgy of the Hours*, 1:528.

30. Ibid., 1:527.

31. *The Forgiveness of Sin* (Chicago: Thomas More, 1979) 121.

32. "A Sermon," *Patrologia Latina. Liturgy of the Hours*, 1:541.

33. Koch, Eugene, "Homily for an Epiphany Priest," *Linking Good News in Ministry* 2 (February 1990).

34. "Sermon," *Patrologia Graeca. Liturgy of the Hours*, 1:577.

35. *A Thief in the Night* (New York: Simon and Schuster, 1989).

36. Antiphon 1, Evening Prayer I, *Liturgy of the Hours*, 1:491.

37. "A Sermon," *Patrologia Graeca. Liturgy of the Hours*, 1:595.

38. Ibid.

39. *Liturgy of the Hours*, 1:1681.

40. "A Sermon," *Patrologia Graeca. Liturgy of the Hours*, 1:595.

41. "From a Commentary on the Gospel of John," *Patrologia Graeca. Liturgy of the Hours*, 1:603.

42. "God's Grandeur," *Liturgy of the Hours*, 1:1681.

43. Ibid.

44. "Sermon on Epiphany," *Corpus Christianorum Series Latina. Liturgy of the Hours*, 1:612.

45. Antiphon 1, Evening Prayer I, *Liturgy of the Hours*, 1:491.

46. *The Sacramentary* (Collegeville: The Liturgical Press, 1985) 513.

47. Ibid., 511.

48. "Sermon," *Patrologia Graeca. Liturgy of the Hours*, 1:634.